Puni

Protecting

The Injustice System
of Family Court

MW00528428

Punished 4 Protecting

The Injustice System of Family Court

Francesca Amato-Banfield

L E O N S M I T H
PUBLISHING
www.leonsmithpublishing.com

Copyright © 2017 Francesca Amato-Banfield

All rights reserved. No part of this book may be reproduced or transmitted in any form or by any means without written permission of the publisher, except in the case of brief quotations embodied in critical articles and reviews.

This material has been written and published solely for educational purposes. The author and the publisher shall have neither liability nor responsibility to any person or entity with respect to any loss, damage, or injury caused or alleged to be caused directly or indirectly by the information contained in this book.

The information in this book is based on the experiences and recollections of the author. These recollections are not intended to be statements of material facts, but rather the author's interpretation of events as they unfolded.

Statements made and opinions expressed in this publication are those of the author and do not necessarily reflect the views of the publisher or indicate an endorsement by the publisher or any of its staff members.

ISBN: 978-1-945446-39-9

Cover photos by:
Photography Gone Green by Vlad Kulpinski

I dedicate this book to my son Christian;
he represents all the children in our country
who are misplaced by judges.

I will never stop fighting for him.

Acknowledgments

The first person I want to acknowledge is my sister, Tonijean Kulpinski. She's one of my greatest supporters and my best friend. She is always there for me. I thank my mother, Adrienne Auchmoody, for always being there for me. My entire family is wonderful: my brother-in-law, Udo; my brother, Richard; my niece, Micheala—who always shops with me—and my sister, Franca. My family suffered tremendously alongside of me during this journey, and I could not have survived without them. To my daughter, Michelle; and my grandchildren, Selah and Elion, I say: *This is for your future.*

I thank my Lord and Savior Jesus Christ. "I can do all things through Him who gives me strength" (Philippians 4:13, NIV)."

I thank my best friend, Kathy Meroney, and my treasured friends for life, Christine Felicello and Jay Hinchman, for all their support and love. I send a very special thanks to dear Angie Wallace, for being an amazing angel in our corner. Without "Aunt Angie," our family would have crumbled.

I also acknowledge all the mothers whom we advocate for and who, in turn, advocate for others. This book is for them, to give them a voice. I want to recognize special advocates Alana Orr, Jessica Erickson, and Jennifer Seekircher, great mothers and tremendous friends. Thanks also to advocate Rosie Caruso.

Two special people who pray for me constantly are my spiritual mothers, Eleanor Seeland and Mary Winchell. A very special prayer warrior who literally held up my arms through this is Dawn Ranco; she blows me away. I can't even describe the support she has given to me.

A very special thank you goes to Jillian Gordon, LCSW, a psychologist and licensed social worker, who goes above and beyond for so many victims and children. Also, I thank a wonderful licensed social worker, dear friend, mandated reporter, and the head of the Tri-State Coalition for Family Court Reform, Victoria Gribbin, LMSW.

I also want to acknowledge Assemblyman Frank Skartados and his chief of staff, Steve Gold, for their tireless work and support.

I thank Steve Pagones and his team at Pagones O'Neill Investigations, and I thank the law firm, MethLaw—Michael Meth and especially Bianca Formisano.

I want to thank my attorney, Steven Klein, our walk-in-and-win guy, who helped me bring my son home and has won for others in a corrupt system.

Finally, I would like to acknowledge the amazing group of people I can now call friends from Leon Smith Publishing. I couldn't ask for a better and more professional team of wonderful human beings. From day one, they were with me through this journey; we laughed and cried together, lifting many prayers to heaven. It blessed me deeply to know Keith, Maura, and Karen were rejoicing together when my son, Christian, returned in September. I learned so much through this process about all that goes into book writing. I can honestly say, "You finished my sentences." I am eternally grateful to Keith and Maura Leon, owners; to Karen Burton, my editor and writing partner; and to Nida, Heather, Dot, and Autumn, members of my publishing team.

Contents

Part I

MOTHERHOOD

Bad News and Good News

I write these words so that my child and I can have a voice. Our story is true, and the truth must be told. The truth is that the family court system in the United States is broken. For almost a decade, I have tried to protect my son while experiencing just how broken the system truly is.

Most of us go through life believing that if we don't do anything wrong, we are safe and so are our children. The bad news is that belief couldn't be farther from the truth. Our family courts across this country fail parents and their children. In fact, our constitutionally secured right to be a parent is violated daily by the entity called *family court*.

When we witness someone struggling with child custody issues, we automatically assume they have done something wrong. This is a myth, a falsehood. I tell my truth to expose how procedural errors and abuse of power are used to manipulate the system and to harm innocent families.

The bad news doesn't end there. Our privacy is being invaded; our civil liberties trampled. Based on my experience, I'd say that most officers of the court and in law enforcement know the system is broken, but they do nothing to correct it. They collect their paychecks and go home each week, knowing that countless children are being endangered by haphazard decisions. These decisions often cause emotional, physical, and sexual damage.

We are in a national crisis.

Do you find it hard to believe this happens?

Or is this happening to you right now?

I have been accused of kidnapping my own child. We have been reported *missing* when we were not. My son and I have been traumatized by decisions made without considering evidence.

Because of my experience, I became an advocate for families seeking to protect their rights and their children. In this role, I have heard countless stories of parents who were dealing first with a failed marriage or relationship and then experienced further failure at the hands of the very courts designed to protect their families. My own lawyers were shocked by the number of articles and true stories I shared with them.

I have years of experience investigating how desperately damaging our system is. I believe it needs more than reform; it needs to be completely abolished!

But there is good news, too.

There is hope. If you are struggling with injustices wrought by our courts, you are not alone. There are resources that will help you. There are advocates to stand with you.

You are not crazy! If you know that you have been doing right for your child all along, do not stop believing that truth. It is your God-given right as a parent to protect your children, and we can stand together to make sure that happens.

My Story

Birth

I gave birth to my son, Christian, in October 2007. I had ended an unhealthy relationship with his father, whom I will call Rick. Rick had a history of addiction to drugs and alcohol and was violent toward me. Christian and I began the work of being a family on our own.

Rick did not visit Christian or support him financially. Imagine my surprise months later, when I received a court date in the mail. I was ordered to appear because Rick had filed for full custody. I remember laughing to myself. I thought: *Yeah, right.* First, Rick was a known drug addict and on perpetual probation from repeated arrests. He had been absent for months.

That court awarded me full custody of Christian and gave supervised visits to Rick. I felt good about this decision and agreed it was the most logical and safest decision for my child and me. I had an order of protection against Rick due to his history of domestic violence.

However, despite his pattern of arrests, drug use, and repeated protection order violations, he continued to take me to court. I do not exaggerate when I say that I was appearing in court about once a month, some months more than once. I was drowning in a flood of legal language and paperwork as my life turned upside down.

How does that happen?

I remember thinking that I shouldn't have to go to court in my entire lifetime as many times as I went during those first years after Rick filed. I was in a revolving door of court. I would show up in my suit and heels. Rick would appear in his dirty clothes from some landscaping job, hair tucked into a baseball cap.

Month after month, we'd face off but we wouldn't speak to each other. Month after month, I showed up and the verdict was the same.

I would drive Christian to supervised visits every week, to a hole of the drug community in Kingston, New York. Week after week, things stayed the same—until Christian was eighteen months old.

New Verdict

What just happened here? I asked myself. We went to court, again. Had a hearing, again. Rick initiated the hearing. My lawyer told the judge that I was uncomfortable with the location of Rick's visits due to drug trafficking at that location. I had suggested a park, a neutral location.

Suddenly, I was standing outside court being informed by my lawyer that Rick had unsupervised visits every other weekend.

"You agreed to it," my lawyer said.

"No, I didn't," I argued. "I didn't say anything at all. How did that happen?"

I hadn't signed anything. I hadn't spoken a word once court began. I had tried to respect the court by keeping my mouth shut. I believed that court was like being pulled over by the police—the appropriate response was to shift into respect mode and keep your mouth shut. Your attorney speaks for you. But mine hadn't spoken *for* me. He had given away my son to a violent, drug-using man four days a month.

I felt abused and invaded. And for the first time, I was afraid. I walked out of court that day with a knot in my stomach, thinking that my son was going to be surrounded by an entire family of drug dealers and addicts.

I Didn't Want to Be There

I began my journey as Christian's mother with an absent father who didn't provide as much as a bottle of water for his care. Every item of clothing, piece of furniture, and ounce of food was provided by me. I was happy to give my child what he needed.

I would never have chosen to fight domestic matters in family court. I was naïve and believed that if I had a good background and provided for my child, my parenting rights were safe. Never in a million years would I have thought that if I went before a judge, my child would be endangered.

Yet, there I was. I went into court as a law-abiding citizen and now was in the fight of my life. I learned a new language, the language of court. I began to research and study law.

I was responsible for driving Christian forty-five minutes each way to his visits. As I moved through these years of unsupervised visits, I tried to support my son every way I could. I sent groceries for the weekend visits to provide him with healthy food. Even though it was only four days a month, my healthy, happy child was suffering the effects of his time with Rick.

Once, he came home with bug bites all over his body. He began talking about *beer* at age four. He also told me that he was sleeping in the same bed as his father and the new girlfriend. Rick drove Christian around without a valid driver's license because he had lost his, due to drunk driving. When my son was six, Rick spent time in jail for domestic violence and violation of orders of protection.

We moved through years with me raising my concerns to a court that never took them seriously. I provided sole support of Christian; Rick still paid no child support.

But I learned. I learned that domestic violence perpetrators will use the court system as part of their abuse. Sharing custody of a child often forces the victim to meet with the abuser, discuss a child's health or school, and keep in contact. Even though I did not have to talk to Rick, I still had to take Christian to visits and see Rick in court. It's sad that children are used by abusers in this way.

It's even sadder that the courts not only allow it, but encourage the continual contact and exposure between parents. More court time means more income for lawyers, judges, and court personnel. It's shocking that this is true, I know. I've had an unfortunate wealth of experience. From these experiences, I have learned about family court throughout our nation, and it is a constitutional anomaly in that it does not reflect the Constitution's purpose.

Family court is one of the most corrupt places in the United States of America. It has endangered the lives of children and violently attacked families. Based on what I have seen, many judges are nothing less than abusers. I advocate they should have mental health evaluations twice a year as they render decisions that often violate human rights. It is horrifying to me that these judges operate without oversight.

I entered Ulster County Family Court in New York as a law-abiding citizen, believing in our justice system. I entered family court not knowing that I would someday be labeled a criminal.

My Family

I came from a family who had never been in trouble. When I think of my grandparents, uncles, aunts, and even great-grandparents, not one of them has ever been arrested or in any sort of trouble, not even a parking ticket. That's the type of family we are—business owners, pillars of the community, respected volunteers. In addition, most of the people I *know* have never been in trouble with the law.

My seventeen-year-old niece is an honor roll student who serves on the board of education for her high school. She's been accepted to every college where she applied. Her top priority in life is her grades. My sister Toni is a holistic practitioner and nutrition expert. I have witnessed clients under her treatment heal from cancer. My mother volunteers for the fire department and the ladies' auxiliary now that she is retired from the hospital.

I have strived to maintain a strong work ethic and an excellent reputation. I am an unwavering advocate. I started my own foundation to help others with similar experiences. I see a need; I try to fill it. That's the kind of person I am. It is also part of my faith, because I know there is hope despite the corruption I've witnessed.

And then, there's my son. Christian is highly intelligent, healthy, creative, and gifted. He remained this way despite the setbacks he suffered during the visits with his father. Every time I would pick him up after a visit, I began the hard work of reversing the damage done during his time with Rick. Every other weekend. Month after month. That's the type of mother I am.

So, the decision of custody should be simple, right?

On the one hand is a father with a bad history, and on the other is a mother in good standing with the law and community. On the one hand is a man mandated to attend AA and NA, and on the other hand is a woman who is raising a healthy, happy child.

Whom would you choose?

Family Faith

My family has faith and strong values. Though faith and values are being attacked in this country, mine have held strong. I thank God for that faith, because I don't know how I would have gotten through this ordeal without it. My faith helps me help other people in similar places.

I don't know how those without faith deal or function when they are in battles for their children. Because this battle was beyond a nightmare.

My child is from a home that is loving, caring, supportive, and safe. When I walked into family court, none of that mattered. The safety and welfare of children should be the very thing taken into consideration. Our laws dictate that's exactly what they should be doing:

> *A parent's right to the preservation of his relationship with his child derives from the fact that the parent's achievement of a rich and rewarding life is likely to depend significantly on his ability to participate in the rearing of his offspring. A child's corresponding right to protection from interference in the relationship derives from the psychic importance to him of being raised by a loving, responsible, reliable adult.1*
> —*Franz v. United States,*
> 707 F.2d 582, 599 (D.C. Cir. 1983)

The Reality

After Rick received unsupervised visits, I felt my power and rights begin to slip away. In family court, *everyone* is treated like dirt, no matter who you are. Before the judge, any person

---

1   For more rulings regarding the rights of parents and children under US law, see the Appendix

can be treated as a criminal, while a person with a criminal history is treated humanely. Stepping into family court is like stepping into the Twilight Zone.

In the rest of the world, I am liked and respected. I am treated civilly. But the moment I walked into court, I entered a barbarian world where rights disappear. I was forced to lower myself down into a pit of hell. The people who work there see it day in and day out, yet most of them do nothing. They see injustice and a system that puts good people in bondage, and they simply collect their paycheck and go home.

Nobody would believe the circus act. It's *pre-decided* when you walk in, like a performance. You expect the justice system, and you get a three-ring circus. And in this crazy world, good people can be labeled *criminal*. I have lived in this circus for nine years and counting.

Slavery and Bondage

When I think of justice, I think of people like Rosa Parks, sitting on a bus seat, demanding her rights. I think of someone like Sojourner Truth, who in the 1800s was the first black woman who *won* from the white man. She won freedom for her children. In fact, they erected a statue to her right here in Ulster County in New York. I find it ironic that the court system is still enslaving people all these years later.

The years of the revolving door into court took their toll on me. I was not allowed to move to a different state. Think about that for a minute: How can anyone living in this free country think this is okay? Fortunately, I was allowed to travel out of state for work and go on vacations without having to ask for permission.

So, if you have a child with somebody and the relationship fails, you are risking not being allowed to move to a different state for eighteen years. Technically, you're on state arrest— it's like being in prison, being a slave. Being mandated to live in-state may limit your ability to better your life or the life of your child. You can't even enjoy the freedoms guaranteed by our Constitution.

Neither judge I dealt with did the right thing. The first judge who presided over my case recused herself in 2016. Then, I found myself under the thumb of Judge Anthony McGinty, a judge who behaved as if he didn't like me and certainly didn't care about the welfare of my child. I couldn't grow, couldn't seek a better job in a different state. I was treated like a common criminal on probation. My entire existence was under the control of one judge. The stress was unbearable.

Family court judges have too much power. They keep people down, so to speak, simply because they choose to do so. No matter who walks into court, whether they be great, law-abiding families or not, they are all treated at a judge's discretion. This is a form of slavery and bondage. This slavery extends to people who are educated and people who have financial means. It extends to people who are assets to their community with a lot to offer their children and everyone else.

For years, people have accepted this imposed slavery. Now, people with businesses find themselves slaves, as do people with master's degrees. Even police officers have told me that they are treated badly despite their uniform and service.

My only crime was protecting my child since the court would not. Imagine, if you will, going to court once a month for nine years to no avail. I walked in with a new police report; I walked out without a change. Rick did jail time. Nothing changed. My record remained clean. Under my care, Christian was happy with an impeccable health record from his pediatrician and holistic health practitioner. He had stability at home.

Rick never completed a domestic violence course or anger management. He threatened me during pick-ups and drop-offs, but there were no consequences. He bought and used drugs. When he got into trouble, I put it in writing. Nothing happened. Nothing.

Yet, I was still moving through this corrupted system, trying to make things work for the sake of my son. I was taking him to his visits and repairing the damage.

I was screaming, "Help me protect my son!"

I was ignored.

Part II

ESCALATION

The Stakes Rise

Unsupervised Visits

I walked a tightrope for the next years, balancing Christian's well-being with the court's demands. He remained a basically happy, healthy boy as he entered kindergarten and first grade. Then, he began to experience trouble at school.

He had always been smart and well-behaved. Now, he was described as hyperactive in the classroom and prone to outbursts. The new court-appointed attorney for Christian, Amy Ingram, was coming to see him at school, and he was being pressured into saying bad things about me. He purposely peed on the toilet. He punched another child.

Suddenly, I was often at school. I talked with his teachers, his counselor, his principal. His behaviors followed a predictable pattern. He would go visit his father, then act out at school for several days. I would work with him to bring him back into balance, and then he would return to his dad.

The school staff walked a fine line, trying not to take sides. They saw the disruption caused by visits with his father, but refused to get involved. They sat on the sidelines while my son was demonstrating the long-term effects of being exposed to Rick's addictions and manipulations. They kept the peace at the expense of my son.

Christian was not old enough to speak to the court. The child attorney lied about his wishes and worked with Rick to manipulate him. He would come home crying and tell me that he felt he had to say what they wanted but he didn't mean it. During this time, we went back to trial for a *year and a half.* That's right, we were in a custody trial for eighteen months. At the end of that trial, nothing changed: I retained custody and Rick was granted unsupervised visits every other weekend.

Christian began to get suspended from school. I was forced to leave my job repeatedly to pick him up or speak with staff. Rick and his girlfriend called Child Protective Services (CPS) to report imaginary problems with me. They harassed me all the time. I took Christian to a therapist. He would cry because *they* wanted him to talk badly about his mother.

When a child is placed in harm's way, they can develop Post-Traumatic Stress Disorder (PTSD). They can experience this disorder at the same level as combat veterans. Children in this circumstance suffer continuous anxiety and fear. Often, their primary caretakers are taken from them, leaving them without the one person who alleviates their fears. Then, children must answer to strangers, who are part of the court system. They are constantly questioned, often being coached on what to say to be a *good* child. All this adds to their stress and damages their psyche.

These children need to be placed back with the people who can heal them, not placed with a dysfunctional parent in a dangerous environment. I knew my son was suffering PTSD and needed protection from its source—the people who were supposed to protect him and uphold the law.

I realized that my son was in true jeopardy. My happy boy was suffering and becoming someone else in front of my eyes. The stress was unbearable. I needed to support him financially, but I was devastated that he was being labeled a *bully* when I knew he was not, not at all. I quit my job and pulled Christian out of public school. I began to home school him. Away from the public institution, he was not available to counselors or attorneys during the day. He began to heal.

Then, I discovered that Rick's brother was dealing heroin. He was caught selling to an undercover cop. I stopped visits altogether because this brother was often at Rick's residence. I went to another court in Orange County and spent four hours getting an order of protection for my son. I felt like I was taking my power back.

I had taken proof of my concerns to McGinty's court and was ignored. I knew I had a right to protect him. I knew. And I knew right from wrong.

The Opposite of Normal

I believe that most healthy parents have an inherent conscience built inside of them to protect their children. It comes naturally. Family court is the extreme opposite of that. It is, I believe, a diabolical institution. For years, it has operated in a wicked manner, answering to no one.

Protective mothers suffer tremendously. These courts and their officials harm innocent people, innocent children. I saw it firsthand. I suffered it firsthand. Perhaps the root cause is the breakdown of the family in our society. Whatever the cause, the *in*justice system is the extreme opposite of normal. A reasonable, decent human being would work to protect a child, to protect the rights of individuals. They do the opposite.

They violate us at their whim, discarding our laws at the federal, state, and local level. They violate everything that is human. This court system polices itself, and they are bullies. It is their way to control people and to generate their own incomes.

There are no juries in family court. There are no cameras. I've sat in many hearings and trials and watched them lead people to believe that they don't have rights.

You may be lead to believe that you don't have any rights.

You have rights.

A parent's right to care and companionship of his or her children are so fundamental, as to be guaranteed protection under the First, Ninth, and Fourteenth Amendments of the United States Constitution.

—In re J.S. and C., 324 A. 2d 90;
129 N.J. Super. 486, 489-492 (1974)

Your rights are guaranteed. Our Supreme Court integrates and protects family court laws and they are nonnegotiable.

God-Given Law

The laws of God are the foundation of who we are as human beings. These laws are found within our country's laws, within our Constitution. They are part of our inalienable rights as human beings, to parent and protect. We are also entitled to this same protection for ourselves. These principles are also found in our health and safety laws. In fact, these basic laws of God for humanity are found in everything we hold dear as a nation.

Since the days of our founding fathers, these laws have governed our lands. These laws have ensured our freedoms and rights which we, as a country, have fought to defend. What these judges do in family court is an utter violation of those laws. They are not legally allowed to take children from people who are fit parents. They are required to follow a due process of law, a trial based on *evidence*, not opinion.

They don't even consider evidence. Instead, they do whatever they want. For years, I provided evidence of Rick's failure as a parent and as a citizen. My evidence was ignored. My civil liberties were denied when this judge refused to consider the truth *in evidence* that was brought into court.

The Declaration of Independence clearly states:

> *We hold these truths to be self-evident, that all men are created equal, that they are endowed by their Creator with certain inalienable Rights, that among these are Life, Liberty, and the pursuit of Happiness. —That to secure these rights, Governments are instituted among men, deriving their just powers from the consent of the governed . . .*

These courts have flipped the intention of the US Constitution. It was the purpose of this new government to ensure that governments (and therefore judges) derive their power from citizens, not the other way around. When these judges act without oversight, when they answer to no one, our rights to pursue a happy life for ourselves and our children are abandoned.

It is up to us to correct this corruption:

> *—That when any Form of Government becomes destructive of these ends, it is the Right of the People to alter it or abolish it . . .*

Rights, therefore, come from God. They are inalienable and the purpose of government is to secure the rights that God gave us. And when government takes our God-given rights, it is time to throw off such government.

The Growing Concern

In the early years of my court battles, the severity of the violations didn't register with me. By the time I had reached this point of pulling Christian out of public school and away from the court's abuses, it was clear that God demanded I protect my child.

If you were taking your child to a babysitter or daycare and they came home talking about drinking alcohol, would you send them back?

Would you allow your first grader to sleep in the same bed with his father and his girlfriend?

I knew these events were serious, and I could not allow them to continue. In my mind, I went back and forth: *Why are they ignoring his arrests? Why won't they consider his continued drug abuse?*

Then, one day a friend called me and told me that Rick was driving around with Christian. I didn't understand her point.

"He is driving around with your son, you know this?" she asked again.

"What are you talking about?" I replied.

"He has multiple DWI convictions and has no license, that's what," she told me.

She was correct. Rick was driving him to drop him off, a forty-five-minute trip.

I brought this event before the judge and Rick admitted it.

When the judge asked Rick how he got to court on that day, Rick admitted it again, "I drove."

The judge did nothing except put in the order that Christian was to have a licensed driver at pick-ups and drop-offs. I sat there baffled. I was astonished.

Is that how you handle his admission?

I was stunned. On the one hand, I knew Christian would be in the car with a licensed driver, and I would get to see their ID. On the other, another illegal activity by Rick was simply ignored.

After this, I would do drop-offs and pick-ups for visits even though I was not required to. Rick often made it difficult to pick up Christian. When I would arrive at the end of the visits, he was nowhere to be found.

More illegal behaviors arose. He again was arrested for domestic violence. His anger and aggression issues escalated. He continued to use and abuse drugs. Finally, one day I was standing downstairs in the family court building and it hit me.

Why am I here? Why am I in this building again?

At this point, I had spent years of my life focused on court dates, arrests, DWIs, drugs, and probation. To top it all off, *Rick never paid a dime of child support during these years.* In that moment, my work as an advocate was born—I realized that I wasn't crazy. I was right and this abuse had to stop.

The Choice I Made

A *Lincoln hearing* was ordered by the judge, but I did not take Christian for evaluation. In these hearings, the child is questioned by the judge while separated from both parents with the attorney for the child present as well. The parents are not allowed to read the transcripts. They ask a child what parent they want to live with.

I don't care if your parents are Hitler and Mother Theresa, you can't ask a child that question. A child should never be put in that position. Also, an abused child is never going to *tell* on their abuser.

He didn't want to go; he begged me to not make him go. He had been so traumatized by all the questions and pressure he had been through. I had a doctor's note saying that he should not attend the hearing as it made him visibly upset. Therefore, I did not make him attend the hearing. Both

Christian and I were diagnosed with PTSD, and the court never granted us ADA accommodations.

We were granted a confidential address by another court, so that Rick could not locate me. I had order of protection *for my son*, protecting him from his father. I already had an order of protection for myself against Rick.

I traveled with Christian; I took him to Pennsylvania. He played tennis and basketball. I worked and vacationed, taking him with me. I sought help for him with professionals who understood the trauma he had suffered. I watched him stabilize, saw him with his smile back again. During this time, the judge knew full well that I was homeschooling my son and was in Pennsylvania.

Seeing this brilliant boy with everything going for him made me feel great, made me feel human again. I took him to music and drawing classes, bringing art back into his life. We visited museums. I watched him grow from writing a sentence on a piece of paper to writing an entire story.

His focus returned now that he was stable and happy. He no longer was being pulled back and forth between two lives, a poor one and a good one. I had no behavioral problems with him at all. I had the son I knew back in my life, and we were happy.

I exercised my God-given right to raise and protect my child. I was in the right, and I still am.

Standing in Faith

Another Story

Once, Christian was almost hit by a car while in Rick's care.

He was only six and was riding his bike with his father. When it was time to cross a highway, Rick went across first. Then, he signaled for Christian to cross on his own. Christian was almost struck by a car. He came home frantic. He wanted to report what had happened to him, so I took him to the police station. He actually told police officers how frightened he was.

Would you allow your six-year-old child to cross a highway by himself? Of course not.

The story frightened me, sickened me. Apparently, it didn't faze Amy Ingram, the court-appointed child attorney.

She was appointed in 2014 to be my son's *attorney for the child* according to New York requirements. From the moment we met, she looked as if she wanted to spit on me. I went up to shake her hand, and all I received in return was hostility.

At the time, I thought it was strange, but there was more to come.

I begged her to recommend supervised visits for Rick, but she didn't listen. She ignored the story about the bike and the car, and then ignored everything else—arrests, protection order violations, inappropriate sleeping arrangements. She became a horror story in my life, and this was the person deemed the protector of my son's rights!

I felt like I was a complete joke to her. I had no voice.

I had no voice.

Testing Times

We all go through situations in life where the proverbial rubber meets the road. These are the moments when we discover if we have faith in God or not. We find the God we've gone to church to learn about and listen to. We remember our fellowship with others and the Word of God, which is true. In these moments, we either believe in the God we have professed or we don't.

In truth, humans can't always help us. We even find ourselves asking: *Why, God, why?*

It is normal to ask this question. The bottom line for me is that I truly believe in God, and He is why I have faith. He gives me peace that I don't really understand. It's not ordinary.

I believe there is scientific proof of God. I have studied the Bible for years and I believe it is scientifically and mathematically perfect. It's bigger than religion. In the end, it's your relationship with Him that allows you to know that He is real and with you. Then, no one else can convince you He is not.

As I struggled through my choices to protect my son, I knew that God was with me. I know that He is with me in the fight today. I know that because I stand in His word, I have a voice, and that voice speaks the truth.

> *For this reason, take up the whole armor of God so that*
> *you may be able to take a stand whenever evil comes.*
> *And when you have done everything you could,*
> *you will be able to stand firm.*
> —Ephesians 6:13, ISV

What does it mean to *stand?*

Standing may seem like doing nothing, but it is an action. It is an action of *knowing.* It is acting in the authority of the truth, girded with the full armor of God as a warrior.

Are you in spiritual warfare? Are you fighting for yourself and your child?

Stand, no matter what happens.

Stand in God and His word.

Stand in truth.

Stand in knowing.

Stand in what is good, what is God.

Stand in belief that He is for you, not against you.

Speak

The devil is a liar and the Bible says that he comes to rob, kill, and destroy. That is what he has done in my situation. He has done this with so many people in this nation through the family courts and other parts of our government. When the entities created to protect us turn and lie to us, steal from us, and seek our destruction—that's evil.

Our world was formed by spoken words. God spoke everything into existence. When we speak the Word, we carry the power of God into the world. No wonder people believe in the power of positive thinking and language. Underneath those current trends is the spiritual law that has always been from the Lord. This law works whether you understand it or not. This law works whether you believe in God or not.

When we see evil, we must speak out against it. We speak the Word, the Scriptures, into the tragic situations we face, and the Truth breaks every lie. That is why it is important to believe.

You must bring that Word to bear in your own situation. It can heal you. When you experience self-doubt, add His power to your circumstance and destroy the work of the enemy against you. No matter what you are dealing with, you can speak the Word.

When I speak the truth, some people tell me *you go too far*, but others say, *you inspire me.*

It is not me that inspires, but the Holy Spirit in me that inspires them. I am a mere person, a person like them, a person like you.

> *Let God be true, and every human being be a liar.*
> *As it is written:*
> *So, that you may be proved right when you speak*
> *and prevail when you judge.*
> —Romans 3:4, NIV

Even when people like Amy Ingram try to silence me, I still have a voice. Even when good parents like you and me are ignored and abused by judges, we still have a voice. We still stand and speak in God's truth.

We are called to take authority in the ungodly kingdoms of this earth that are not of God. It is God's desire to bless us with health and prosperity for our whole families. In our world, it is easy to see that the devil has stolen this blessing from people. We have removed God from everything. We have moved away from Him. We have left the truth. And therefore, we suffer the consequences.

It takes a warrior to go forward and break the silence. It takes faith.

Part III

THE INJUSTICE SYSTEM

Patterns of Practice

There is nothing *family* about family court.

Endangering the welfare of children and re-victimizing victims is the standard pattern of practice for these courts. Judges, child attorneys, and public defenders are abusive bullies using courts as their arena. Here, they wreak havoc on families with no semblance of judicial integrity.

We watch news reports about barbaric courts in other countries. We see images of inhumane conditions and practices, such as children being sold on the streets into sex slavery. We know there are places in this world where bribery and corruption are the everyday practice of officials. We shake our heads in disgust.

Yet, here in the United States, we believe everything is polished and civilized. Our courts have the look and guise of professionalism, of decency. Yet their practices are as barbaric as the ones we shake our heads at on the news. It's the same picture, just framed differently.

Alice's Story²

I met Alice in my travels as an advocate. She told me that she has not seen her daughter for two years. She reported sexual abuse of her daughter, and now, she has orders of protection filed against *her*. She has not threatened anyone and does not deserve these court orders. These court orders are a form of retaliation.

She took her daughter to doctors and professionals who confirmed her reports in writing. These professionals contacted CPS as mandated by law. What happened? Nothing. The entire situation went flat as if it had never happened.

She represents hundreds of parents—parents who report sex abuse, parents who struggle to remove their children from the possession of persons on a sex offender registry. She was dismissed along with countless others by court officials who simply say, *he couldn't have abused his own child, or he's an okay guy.*

Women Are Treated Like Liars

If you search the internet, you can find dozens of articles that claim that women make up stories of abuse as a means of getting what they want—another falsehood. It's a small

---

2   * Names and logistics in this section have been changed to protect individual identities.

fraction of women who actually lie about domestic violence. In fact, less than 2 percent of women who are custodial parents lie about abuse.[31] Usually, there is a mountain of evidence alongside these claims—black eyes, PTSD, fractures. This evidence can be even more blatant, such as arrests, protection order violations, or probation. The courts ignore the evidence, thus treating these women as liars.

Sometimes, women will back away from their reports of abuse out of fear for themselves or of losing their children to abusers. Thus, they are re-victimized by the court system that was put in place to protect both the child and mother.

I started out as *pro-parent*. I listened to women who shared their stories and evidence of domestic violence, *and* I also advocated for men who are good fathers. Now, I consider myself *pro-family,* and I believe that removing a fit dad or mom from a child's life is child abuse in and of itself.

Jennifer's Story

Another woman I met in my journey was beaten in front of her children. She entered family court, only to have the family twist the story. A situation that should have been obvious— cut and dried—turned into a nightmare. Her children were taken from her and given to her abuser.

---

3   [1] Faller, Kathleen. 2006. False accusations of child maltreatment: A contested issue. Child abuse & neglect. 29. 1327-31. 10.1016/j. chiabu.2005.10.002.

The court acknowledged the ongoing dysfunction of the perpetrator and then refused to turn the situation around. This decision causes further damage to the children the mother was trying to protect. Now, she has no means of protecting them.

Jennifer also represents hundreds of parents. Her story could be the story of so many other wounded people suffering not only for themselves, but for their children.

Gambling with Children

The issue before us is not law reform. The laws we need are already in place, along with our basic rights. What demands reform are the judges, the child attorneys, and the case workers who make decisions in vacuums with no oversight. Often, a decision that will affect the life of a child forever is rendered in four minutes after reading one transcript.

Any business in this country must conform to health and safety laws. Fast food restaurants must follow strict codes for cleanliness and for the handling of food. Day care centers are routinely inspected to ensure that the children are cared for properly and safely. Even our public parks are routinely checked and monitored so that we can enjoy them without fear and worry.

Not so in our family courts. Routinely, a background check is done to see if there is an order of protection. No other sort of background check is conducted. If any other evidence is offered or testimony given, it is at the sole discretion of the judge to believe or act on it. Even in the case of the orders of protection, the judge may ignore them.

I am living proof of this fact: I have *never* had an order of protection against me, and Rick has *always* had one against him.

The dice are rolled with precious futures and sometimes their very future is lost.

Saddest of Outcomes

Here in my home state of New York, a little boy was murdered. His mother allowed her new boyfriend to move into their home and left the boy while she went to look for work. Every day, she would come home to a child covered with external bruises. He was sexually abused and his rib cage broken. He suffered internal injuries. Eventually, he was beaten to death.

She didn't call for help. She ignored over sixty bruises on her own child. This woman was cleared by the Ulster Family Court of any wrongdoing. Yet, I know women who have been arrested simply for protecting their children, including myself.

Remember when I said this entire system was the opposite of normal? I can't count how many mothers were sent to jail for protecting their children.

Can you say *backward?*

The Wrong Parent

Placing a child into the hands of someone who is a perpetrator of domestic violence is the wrong choice. If you have ever been assaulted by another person, I know you understand this statement. People who cannot control their anger will continue to lash out in violence. Children in this environment are directly exposed to violence and all the fear and anxiety attached to it.

Placing a child in the care of somebody who doesn't have a job or pay child support is another wrong choice. This endangers the child's welfare in terms of proper nutrition, healthcare, and life necessities.

Placing a child with someone whose history is full of perpetual probation or parole is the wrong choice. Children need and deserve role models. They are learning to make their own life decisions and choices. They deserve a life that is free of worry about arrests and prison sentences.

When a child is placed with the wrong parent, that child is being endangered whether they see the parent during unsupervised visits or for full custody. Not only are they experiencing violence and a lack of resources in a bad environment, they are being deprived of the healing presence of the safer parent—the parent who values the child's welfare and works toward their happiness.

A child should be placed with the parent who supports the child, protects the child, nurtures the child.

Why would anyone do anything else?

Diana's Story

A dear advocate and excellent mother learned that her ex, with whom she shared a child, had been dishonorably discharged from the Navy for child pornography. After visits with the father, she noted evidence of sexual abuse and regression issues. Four separate medical professionals verified her complaints. Judge McGinty, in Ulster County, gave sole custody to Diana's parents, which was bizarre and unlawful.

He robbed the mother of her child and the child of her mother. This child no longer has the only safe place she ever knew. It's been two years as I write this. This judge and the same child attorney assigned to Christian have abused this mother and violated her rights. The sex offender is allowed unfettered access to the child. The judge refuses the mother's pleas for help.

Money-Making Scam

As I see it, this entire crisis all comes down to money. Money is made through incentives. Legislators ask me how money is made if the court is filled with public defenders and the people are poor. They want to know how are these judges making money.

The judges in Ulster county make $160,000 a year on your tax dime and state funding.

How are they making money by postponing rendering decisions?

It's quite simple. They are stealing taxes from the taxpayer. And they dole out work to public defenders like candy, so money continues to funnel through the system. The longer they keep a case in their revolving door, the more they make. They keep families in chaos, because chaos means more cases.

Conflict is generated by stretching out cases over longer periods of time, stressing the persons involved. High conflict means more state funding because now CPS, law enforcement, and more court dates are needed. One father I know lives in a home worth $400,000 and he has a public defender. I may not understand all the details of funding, but I know something about this isn't right.

They intentionally don't solve cases. The corruption is based in financial gain, and let's face it: *The love of money is the root of all evil* (I Tim 6:10, KJV). No one in their right mind would intentionally render decisions that harm children if they didn't have something personal to gain, such as more money.

Federal and state funding are involved in keeping the family court going. Then, the officers of the court complain that they can't render decisions because of case overload. *That is the biggest bunch of nonsense I've ever heard.* Why? You don't have to be a judge or have half a brain to decide what is safe or what is not.

As advocates, we have designed a way to do just that, and I will share more about that later.

The Villains

Public Defenders

We call them *public pretenders* in my court in Ulster County, New York. They are just robbing people—robbing the taxpayers. They are paid through state funding and are distributed to people freely. People don't have to be indigent; they don't have to be poor. It doesn't matter. Judges prefer to assign them because they work *for* the court.

I have found them to be phonies and liars. They want to hear your story so they can encapsulate it in lies, keeping it within their boundaries. They say they will help you. They do not. They don't do anything at all except conserve the diabolical, financial stealing of taxpayers' money.

It's a systemic problem, because they all work together. They destroy families and continue to collect their paychecks. They don't work for you. They do not represent you. They work for the court.

To them, it's in and out, like a fast-food chain with a revolving door. There have been moments when I have actually wondered if they are human. They are conscious, so I know there must something human inside them. Maybe they are a hybrid species, something else. How else could they sleep at night?

The difference between a paid lawyer and public defender is like eating at the Waldorf Astoria and McDonald's. You don't go to a fast food restaurant to get the nutrition your body needs; you go to a health food store. If you settle for fast food, you're going to get nothing of the kind of stuff you need.

Andrew Gilday

Rick has had the same public defender, an aggressive man who would defend Rick for murder if need be. Once, I requested a forensic evaluation of Rick's mental state. When we got to court, the public defender stood up all hot-headed and demanded one for me.

Mr. Gilday has an Uber driver bring him to court. He is disrespectful. It was during the trial that he yelled at me and did a song and dance in the court room.

He was very theatrical, mocking me and saying, "What is she talking about her God-given right? What does she mean her God-given right?"

This is what I mean when I call family court a circus act.

Attorneys for the Child

In 2009, the state of New York established a new law that children in family court are to be assigned child attorneys, replacing the former child advocates. According to the New York state government web site, the "role of the attorney for the child is to serve as the child's lawyer. The attorney for the child has the responsibility to represent and advocate the child's wishes and interests in the proceeding or action."[42]

The law makes sense when you read it, but the courts are full of attorneys who are not versed in domestic violence and child abuse. They only make bad situations far worse. Children are fearful and eager to please at the same time. They are easily damaged by pressure to choose or answer *correctly*.

Amy S. Ingram

Apparently, family court in Ulster County did not realize it was supposed to appoint child attorneys instead of child advocates. For many years, Christian had a child advocate who listened to me and advocated for what he called *the best interest*. While I don't believe anyone in the court system really works for this *best interest*, he did advocate for the safety of my child. I begged him for supervision for Rick during his visits, but the pattern of unsupervised weekends went on.

---

4   [2]nycourts.gov/courts/ad4/AFC/AFC-ethics.pdf

Then, in 2014, Amy Ingram was appointed as Christian's attorney for the child. I mentioned before that she was hostile the first time we met. This woman would go to school to talk to my child and grill him with questions.

He would cry because of the guilt he had inside.

"Mommy, Mommy, I feel so bad but he (Rick) would make me say I want to live with him but I don't. He would make me tell that to Amy."

I would say, "When you get in there, you tell the truth."

"No, because he would be mad at me; he would be mad at me. He would get angry with me."

He shared this with his therapist and we have it documented. Amy Ingram knows this. But this woman stood up in court and argued that a drug addict should have access to my son. She fought vehemently for Rick to get full custody. She ignored all the domestic violence, drug addiction, jail time for abuse, lack of child support, and ongoing probation violations.

She lacks proper training in the effects of domestic violence and abuse. She has a terrible reputation because of her lack of a conscience. Apparently, she doesn't understand that children are fearful and easily damaged by the stress of being forced to choose.

Remember Diana, whose ex-husband was discharged from the Navy for child pornography? Guess who serves as her child's attorney? Amy Ingram. She also served as the attorney for the mother who allowed her son to be beaten to death but was found not guilty of negligence. The facts speak for themselves.

Judges

Judges in family court rule supreme in their own worlds. No cameras or juries are present in their courtrooms. They are granted wide discretion in the rendering of decisions. They have no accountability either. They are not required to have any physical or mental examinations to remain on the bench.

In their world, they reign. If a judge doesn't like you, you are never going to win. Your rights don't matter. Your children's safety is gambled on a four-minute decision rendered often without evidence.

The judges are at the top of the chain. They are often appointed by politicians and re-elected without opposition. They assign public defenders as they please. They treat people like garbage whenever they want.

Judge McGinty

Anthony McGinty is the supervising judge for Family Court of Ulster County in New York state. He was elected to the bench in 2005, and ran unopposed in the 2015 election for a second ten-year term.

When Rick first took me to court, a different judge was assigned our case. In March 2016, she recused herself from our case, and we were assigned to McGinty. I joined a group of women who have all suffered in his courtroom. His pattern of violating the rights of parents, particularly mothers, goes back years.

He targets moms. The behavior and speech I've witnessed leads me to believe he hates women for some reason. He has taken many children from their mothers and given them to abusive fathers. He has removed visitation from women with good backgrounds who were never found unfit. Then, the woman whose child was beaten to death was let off the hook.

The mothers who have suffered in his court share a similar story of having impeccable backgrounds. They suffered and complained about domestic violence. This treatment is a direct violation of rights.

This judge still sits there and makes decisions, wreaking havoc on families.

Months before the mother was scheduled to appear in court, I happened to be standing out in the hallway of the court building after a meeting with my lawyer and overheard that the mother was not going to be found negligent. The people talking in the hall were correct. The decision was already made, but hadn't been *tried* in a courtroom. The father would get custody, the boyfriend would go to jail, but the mother would not see a jail. I sent an email recounting that I had heard the result before the decision was *public,* but nothing happened until the appeals court heard the case.

In the case of the murdered child, however, his decision to release the mother without responsibility was challenged. The Appellate Division of the Supreme Court of New York concluded "that Family Court erred in dismissing the severe abuse petition against . . . (the mother)." They listed the reasons as obvious bruising and an injury that would have caused vomiting blood.[53]

Justice Looks Like . . .

A just court would consider what is in the best interest of a child—safety, protection, and a loving home. Every child needs a home in which they'll be taken care of properly. When a judge sees that there is any kind of conflict in a home, they should make a good decision and safeguard the child, which is the right thing to do.

If a parent has anger issues and is guilty of domestic violence, they should be required to take parenting and anger management courses. They should be held accountable for completing these classes. They should show that they have

---

5 [3]Case #521140, decisions.courts.state.ny.us

actually improved their lives to make them a more suitable parent. Then, and only then, should a child be merged back into the lives of both parents, if it's workable.

Unless parents are held accountable to complete improvements, they usually won't. It's sad to say that it won't always work for both parents to stay in the life of the child.

If these issues were addressed in the beginning of a custody dispute, then proper investigations could be done with evidence collected and handled in a proper manner. Instead, judges' decisions turn a situation that could have a positive result into utter chaos. They pour kerosene on the fire. Then, there is a blaze that could have been avoided with proper process at square one.

Our judges should be rendering decisions that are in the best interest of the children. That terminology, though, is just a bunch of mumbo-jumbo court talk. It has become another part of the whole pseudo-court system that exists to generate more and more money.

Additionally, all our court officers—judges, public defenders, attorneys for children—should have mandated mental health exams to keep honesty in this broken system.

CPS—Child Protective Services

According to Child Protective Services, if they come into a home and a child is being punched, that action would be an *indication* of maltreatment and abuse, of inadequate guardianship. These indicators might result in taking that child away from that family. Their intention begins in the right place.

CPS is part of the same system as the judges and courts. They receive their funding from the same place. Sometimes a report is filed, and then CPS doesn't do anything because the family is in a *custody* battle right now. That's one problem. Another problem is CPS indicating people while they are in custody battle so it continues to prolong the court hearings, thus generating more and more money.

In the end, case workers and CPS officials all answer to the judges, who answer to no one. It's a vicious cycle.

Part IV

STAND

Nowhere to Turn

In 2014, I started thinking about the years I had endured, and I decided it was time to do something about it. I started contacting legislators. I did everything I could think of and parents started coming out of the woodwork.

I would hold a meeting and people would pour in. They came from New York, but also from New Jersey and Connecticut. This was during the time when the boy upstate was murdered. We all believed this tragedy would change the patterns of abuse, but it didn't. I began to research our laws. I discovered my rights to parent and to protect. I discovered my God-given rights in the Family Court Act and in the Constitution of the United States.

The Journey

We'd been to the district attorney's office. We had compiled tons of evidence and given it to people who literally sat on their rear ends and did absolutely nothing. They told me they had no jurisdiction. They thought we were fools.

We went to the FBI. We've been on the news. We've held rallies. There is not a person, there is not a sheriff's department, there's not a state trooper we have missed in our contacts and sharing of evidence.

We talked about the children. We told stories of sex abuse, physical abuse, and violence. They are all so well informed by us that they are in violation of New York State penal code 260.10, which makes it illegal to endanger the welfare of children.

The Department of Justice told us that they did not have enough funding.

I found myself asking: *Where is the punch line to this sick joke? Are they kidding?*

We went through the entire gamut of scheduling appointments and meeting times. We discussed everything. We showed paperwork and evidence. They acted as if they were going to do something about it. And basically, they laughed at us as we walked out the door. They did nothing. Nothing.

State Senator

We invited a state senator to a meeting. He did not show up, but sent his personal secretary. She wept during the meeting as we discussed the results of the autopsy on the murdered child. She was aware of what was going on, and she tried to do her job. But this senator did absolutely nothing.

I know he could have done something. He is under a moral obligation to the welfare of the children in his district. So, when he says there is nothing he can do, I leave it to you, the reader, to decide if you really believe that.

The Media

I held a Rally for Reform in front of the courthouse and another rally following the death of the little boy. We drew the media. Our rally was on TV pretty much all day. It made the papers and local news reports. But then, the media stopped returning my calls. I suspect that they were contacted by someone from Family Court. Maybe they were threatened.

We wrote letters and newspapers refused to publish them. It makes me wonder who paid whom. Why would anyone not report on our efforts?

Attorney General

The attorney general in New York is a complete joke. He's received hundreds of letters and emails and calls. He did absolutely nothing. And he said the same thing, "We're sorry, we don't have jurisdiction."

So, again, I leave it up to you, the reader, to research our country and see if our attorneys general have no jurisdiction over our laws and rights. Especially when they have a little department called *Public Integrity*. What an oxymoron!

There is no integrity when public servants endanger the welfare of victims, the welfare of children.

A Friend?

My mother ran into an acquaintance from her school days who works for the Ulster County district attorney's office. They were at the post office. She asked him to help ensure that my son and I would be safe in our town. She told him that a missing persons report was filed in error against us and that I was innocent even though I had a warrant out for my arrest—a story I will share in the next section.

His response was basically, "Well, when you do a crime . . ." He had known my mother for years, yet talked about me as if I were a criminal. He knew that both she and my family had clean records. In fact, he had previously gone light on Rick in legal matters, making life even more difficult for my son and me. He was part of the domino chain moving us in this nightmare.

His actions show the wickedness in some people and how they buy into a system. In situations like this one, you can see people for who they really are. My mother confronted him and told him that he was not doing justice, not doing the right thing. He came face to face with the truth and turned away.

Commission on Judicial Conduct

From June to October of 2016, I compiled information on seventy victims, including pictures, medical records, and arrest records. I had pictures of children with burn marks and evidence of sexual abuse. I had pictures of blood in diapers and punch bruises from beatings. It was sent directly to the Committee on Judicial Conduct. I can't tell you exactly where it was sent, because it was sent by someone in the district attorney's office.

We cc'd everything to a law firm. We sent copies to other advocates. We documented what we call a *pattern of practice* that we were witnessing.

Their response? No judicial malpractice here.

We are talking about major forms of abuse: emotional, physical, and sexual abuse. And they found no misconduct. How is that logically possible? It felt as if we had nowhere to turn.

My Coalition

Emergency Status

Have you ever experienced an emergency with your child?

Medical emergencies are handled in emergency rooms.

What happens if you are involved with family court?

Let's say your child is visiting and tells you something about their weekday life that makes your heart stop. You are terrified to send your child back. It's the weekend, the time of your scheduled visit. Family court is not open on the weekends.

What do you do?

If you go to the police, and they learn you're involved in family court, they will refer you to family court, no matter how serious the issue is. So, you take off work on Monday to file an emergency petition. Then, the court assigns you a court date. Remember, *this is an emergency.*

Then, you finally get to the court date, and they don't take evidence that day. Remember, this was an emergency.

They do a prehearing. All the while, your child is back in a dangerous situation, and you are living in constant fear.

This limbo time endangers children.

On the other hand, if you call your local fire department because a cat is up the tree, they come running and take that cat down. They don't have to file a paper; they don't have to conduct an investigation. That cat has more protection and safety than a child.

Local Coalition

I finally realized that we are in a crisis—an emergency—as a country. I decided to get involved. I met Vicky Gribbin, LMSW, the founder of the Tri-State Coalition for Family Court Reform. She works in Long Island, Connecticut, and parts of New Jersey. Vicky is a reporter, social worker, and a retired New York City police officer. She is a mandated reporter and a forensic domestic violence expert. She has extensive knowledge about what's happening in family courts. She also has extensive knowledge on disability rights and legal rights.

She made me the chapter leader for Ulster County, New York. I've been working with this coalition since 2013. We work with court advocates and other advocacy groups.

I brought Vicky to a closed-door meeting with Assemblymen Frank Skartados and other experts. I even invited attorneys who were on the right side. We made a plan after the child was murdered upstate, thinking that this was a time to act.

We had held our rally and been on the news. As I said before, that didn't last and things did not improve.

I did start to learn all the family stories. I've listened to mothers whose children have come back with cigarette burns in their arms. I've seen the pictures of the deep wounds. I've seen medical reports of sexual abuse that were completely ignored, hundreds of stories from all over this country.

We did background checks on the people who came to us and found out that they were fine, but their children were being placed in danger repeatedly. I mean, story after story. I stood in this truth for years.

I did everything I could to spearhead from Ulster County. Vicky was in her own court case in Long Island. Finally, I realized that we are part of a movement of thousands upon thousands strong who are standing against what is happening. I decided to branch off.

Advocacy Work

So, I *court watch*. I take my clipboard and take notes. I watch for illegal violations of a person's civil liberties or constitutional rights. I write down any time a good parent loses their parental rights or has them questioned. When they tell the judge they haven't seen their child for x-amount of time, I make a note. I stand with good parents, and I am a witness that the judge knows the truth of the situation. We have a huge mountain that needs to be knocked down, and we are documenting every piece that we can.

As advocates, we spend the time necessary to evaluate each case and get to know the people involved. We do background checks on everyone we advocate for. We get to know them and their family members. This process is not difficult. If we go to a home and see beer bottles everywhere, there might be an issue. We know this is not a family we really want to represent.

It's not hard to get to know people. We visit grandparents and parents and see the child in their care. When the child looks healthy and happy, loved and cared for, it is not difficult to see where they belong.

The courts make it difficult, because the courts are broken. The entire system is broken. And how does a broken system expect to fix a broken family? They cannot do it.

My hope is that eventually, when our coalition is big enough, we will go into court as mediators. Our name will carry so much power and truth that when we stand by a parent, we will help them win their case. We will do such a thorough job of investigations and background checks that anyone we advocate for will be known as a good parent. That is my vision.

National Coalition

I started receiving calls from people around the nation, so I turned my coalition into a national one. I formed the National Coalition Family Court and CPS Reform in 2014. I added CPS to it, so that we can have advocates and chapter leaders in every county and every state. So, I started my own group and continued working with Assemblyman Skartados and his chief of staff, Steve Gold.

I learned that some states are just as bad as New York. California is really bad. Connecticut is really bad and so is West Virginia. Minnesota is horrible and especially bad to women who are victims of domestic violence. Some states are clearly against dads and others are against mothers.

CPS needs a different demeanor, a basic respect for everyone to be treated as a human being. It should be easy and simple to discuss laws and situations that affect a family. Case workers should be willing to work to de-escalate conflict as quickly as possible, so that the family does not have to endure long periods of trauma.

It is important that we work together to make people understand that dotting the *I*s and crossing the *T*s needs to be done, especially by the government. We need to be articulate and do proper assessments.

I believe if we can accomplish this in New York, it will become an example state for the rest of our nation.

This problem affects our whole country. Here's the thing. The United States has a problem with the terrorist group known as the Islamic State of Iraq and Syria (ISIS), right? They are *terrorists*, after all. However, ISIS doesn't affect every single home in our nation.

Family Court affects every single home in our nation.

If it's not affecting you, it's affecting your neighbor, it's affecting your friend, your cousin, your nephew, or your grandchild. To me, family court is genuinely a terrorist group in our country, inflicting damage on children and their parents, every single day.

Let the Games Begin

Rick and I went back to trial in 2016. The trial was scheduled to start in November. In September, I got a knock on my door one evening at seven o'clock. It was a CPS worker, coming to investigate a report filed on me. This is how the game began.

At this point, I had become an outspoken advocate, reaching out to a national community. Other advocates warned me that CPS would soon be coming after me. Sure enough, they worked with my son's father, public defender, and child attorney. These people would call CPS, who would come knocking on my door even though nothing was ever found on me.

This went on. I had five separate complaints called in against me within a year and a half. You can decide if it is a coincidence that my trial with Rick also lasted a year and a half.

To be honest, one indication was found against me. CPS showed up, following up on a call made by Rick against me. They filed a report that was so accurate it was under the name *Mr.* Amato with a Kingston, New York address. Rick's address was on the report, even though they came to my home in Marlboro. So, that goes to show you how CPS does or doesn't do their job. And, I had to overturn that blip on my record myself, which I did. CPS apologized all the way up to the judge.

Things were put in writing by mistake. However, if someone read them or just looked at those things, I could look really bad.

Then, I started working with the district attorney's office on the calls. Every call that came in after that, I reported the false CPS allegations, which are a crime. The DA's office had extensive information on the calls; they knew there were five in a row. Even Ulster County refused to take the calls any longer. Yet, Rick was not arrested for harassing me.

Your taxpayer dollars were hard at work sending CPS workers after me, keeping them from doing their job of protecting children.

Part V

PUNISHED

The Time Between

Rescue

Imagine you are at a lake, enjoying a picnic with your child on the shore. There are signs posted everywhere: *No swimming under penalty of law*. Your child wanders away and falls into the water. Immediately, they are in distress, flailing their arms and crying for help.

What do you do?

You jump into the water and save your child's life. In that moment, there is no question about whether to break the law. But soon, you are going to jail for swimming in the lake.

This is what the family court does. I am living proof.

New Start

Once I decided to stop Christian's visits with Rick, I took steps to protect us. I moved to another court outside of my home county and filed for an order of protection for my son. It was granted, and for the first time in the nine years since his birth, we *both* had orders of protection against Rick. Then, I applied for a confidential address in every state in which I worked and traveled. This confidential address granted me the right to keep my physical location private and unavailable.

I traveled with my advocacy work and vacationed some with my son. I took back the reins of raising my child. He was not jumpy; he wasn't nervous. He didn't bully anyone. He wasn't being abused or exposed to violence and drugs. He was in a safe environment.

I was no longer a victim. It was wonderful. I stopped everything—the CPS calls, the questions, the nonsense. I saw the signs of PTSD reverse in Christian. His injuries from the emotional abuse and trauma were healing under my care. PTSD is not a mental illness; it is an injury. In a safe environment with love and support, injuries can heal.

One court told me I needed to designate someone, and I was too stressed to argue. I had been there four hours already and was programmed after nine years of court to bow down to what they say. I had a bad feeling about picking someone as a contact, but I chose my mother. I can remember thinking: *I can have a confidential address in all these other places. Why do I have to give my mother's address?* They never told me that this person would receive official mail or be served for me.

Now, I have learned that you shouldn't bow down.

You should always say, "Wait a minute."

I don't know how victims of serious domestic violence handle the stress of being told everything they can and can't do. They are already afraid to speak for themselves because they have been brutalized for doing that. They are afraid to fight back.

So, some man came banging on my mother's door at six o'clock in the morning and walked into her house. He walked into my niece's bedroom, posing as a process server. He asked for me.

My mother told him, "Fran isn't here. Fran doesn't live here."

Then she saw a paper with Rick's name on it, so my mother told him to take a hike. He was rude and unprofessional. So, my being served was screwed up because my mother was terrified. We didn't even realize that I was being served about a court date.

All I cared about at that time was the healing journey I was taking with my son.

Documenting the Damage

In the 2014 trial for custody, I called a domestic expert, Barry Goldstein, to the stand. He educates judges about the Adverse Childhood Experiences (ACE) score and the Saunders Study. The judge completely ignored what he had to say. But ACE scores are recognized by the Center for Disease Control and Prevention. The factors scored have tremendous impact on the child's adult life—violent behavior and victimization, depression, and even life expectancy.

As such, early experiences are an important public health issue. The experts consider traumatic situations that a child experiences, including those suffered in the midst of domestic violence, and assign a score to them. If a child is physically hit, the score goes higher. When a child is taken from a primary caregiver, the score goes off the chart because it harms their brains, causes trauma, and shortens their life. Mr. Goldstein has written books on the subject, but the court ignored him, completely.

During this time, I took Christian to several professionals for evaluation and therapy. Several events in his life counted as ACEs, such as seeing domestic violence, hearing his mother bad-mouthed around the clock, and being forced to tell the child attorney he didn't want to live with me. These adverse experiences caused his outbursts in school—every Monday after a visit. I had known that my son needed protection, and now I had more evidence of the damage being done by putting him in a dangerous environment.

All I could think was: *How dare you!*

I also went to see professionals for myself. I was reminded about the Saunders Study, in which researchers studied domestic violence and what lawyers and judges believe about it. They talked about how courts need to know that abused women suffer mental health problems, especially after years of abuse. If a woman is depressed or suffering PTSD, officials will hold that against her in the custody hearing when it's the abusers fault that she's that way. I was diagnosed with PTSD and other issues resulting from years of abuse.

The study also found that if people have training about domestic violence, they don't usually think the victims are making stuff up or trying to hurt the children. I don't understand how child attorneys and judges can render decisions that break lives without even having this training.

Not too long ago, someone asked me why Rick wanted custody in the first place. I didn't have an answer. He didn't visit Christian. He didn't support him. In fact, he didn't pay any child support until his paycheck was garnished when Christian was eight years old.

The Saunders Study has an answer: "Abusers use any portion of legal custody as a way to continue harassment and manipulation through legal channels."[64] The perpetrators start the abuse and the courts keep it going and going to line their pockets.

This time was healing for me, too. Going to court was like getting punched in the stomach over and over again. I would have to build myself up for the days before. Then, I would be calm in the courtroom. Afterward, I would be physically sick for three days.

We had both been through so much, but neither of us knew the worse hadn't happened yet.

---

6   [4]ncjrs.gov/pdffiles1/nij/grants/238891.pdf

Retaliation

Missing

I thought we would be protected by our confidential address and orders of protection. In May 2016, Judge McGinty revoked the order of protection for my son that I had spent hours obtaining in Orange County. My PTSD shot through the roof. At this time, I had no attorney and was alone in court.

I asked the judge, "How can you do this? Didn't you see the evidence?"

He replied, "It's my court. I'm the judge."

I kept protecting my bear. That was that. I am a mother and I protect my child. What else is a mother to do? When you attack my child, you are crossing God-given lines. I continued, helping him recover and heal. We continued to travel as I homeschooled him with the court's complete knowledge.

From June to October of 2016, I was working with the district attorney, compiling evidence against the judge. In December, I heard a rumor that there was a warrant for my arrest. I couldn't believe it was true.

That DA kept saying, "We will push it back. Don't worry. Get a lawyer, get a lawyer, get a lawyer . . . "

The warrant kept getting pushed back and pushed back and pushed back by the DA's office. I spend time on the phone with a chief investigator, and we tried to figure things out. I still wasn't served with any paperwork, and I still wasn't looking at an order. Christian and I kept living our lives.

I secured a law firm at the advice of the DA. We were working together to find a solution. They were pointing out all the holes, all the retaliation, all the abuse, everything. The wheels were turning slowly.

Then, in late December, Rick reported us *missing* to the Missing Persons Clearinghouse of New York. This clearinghouse was formed to help locate people who are vulnerable or at risk. He began going all over town, posting flyers with pictures of us. Rick was driving around without a license, putting signs up. He was asking for information about our whereabouts, implying that the boy was in danger from his custodial parent.

Hundreds of people called the Missing Persons Clearing-house saying that we were *not* missing but were victims of domestic violence. They told them that the boy was not in danger from his mother. Everyone in my family and community was running around, ripping down signs. They were pissed off and angry, tired of seeing what we see in this country.

The big kicker is that I talked to the court secretary on the very day the missing persons report was being filed. My retained counsel had ordered transcripts from the secretary to discover what had happened. I was not in town, but I was not missing.

Rick used this tactic just to locate us.

It didn't seem to matter that people were calling and saying, "I know this mother takes care of this child, and your organization is wrong."

The Clearinghouse would ask the callers if they knew where I was, and they would say no because they didn't know. I had a *confidential* address. I was on this list for a short time, just enough time to wreak havoc on my family and friends.

My mother felt threatened and was visited by the police many times. The police were wonderful to her, but one time they came at two o'clock in the morning. The district attorney and police lieutenant put a stop to that. They actually stopped them from going to my mother's house any more.

Then, something appeared on Facebook saying that Rick has been given full custody of Christian. I have Rick's family blocked on Facebook, but the information made its way around. I read that the judge had actually written in the order, ". . .although the father is problematic with a convicted criminal history and drug addiction, he is the more suitable parent." I *knew* that couldn't be true.

Could it?

My son was playing outside and kids were saying, "You are going to have to live with your dad and your mom is going to jail." The kids were innocent, not intending to be mean. I told Christian it was going to be okay.

According to Judge McGinty, I was properly served and failed to appear. Rick was granted sole custody of Christian, and when I failed to produce Christian—I didn't know, of course—a warrant was eventually issued for my arrest.

In response to this news, my son began falling apart. One day, we went to Walmart because he wanted an action figure. I noticed something. My son is a typical boy. He runs into aisles, picks out toys, shows me things. This kid was squeezing my hand so tight. I noticed it. He would not let go of me, even when we got to the aisle. He was picking up stuff with the other hand. Looking at it with one hand instead of two hands. And just holding me.

Then, my son told me he had been touched inappropriately by his ten-year-old cousin. Talk about heartbreaking. His stress score rocketed to the level of a Vietnam veteran, according to ACEs.

The Worst Day

I was visiting in DC as an advocate and staying in West Virginia. Christian had told me about his cousin touching him inappropriately during a visit. The psychiatrist I was seeing reported this event as she is mandated to do.

I received a call from my friend who lived around the corner from where we were staying and was watching Christian while I was away. "I think you better get here right now. The police are here, and Christian slammed and locked the door. I let them in, but he's telling everybody, 'I don't want to go with my dad, I don't want to go with my dad.'"

The police had blocked my friend's car when they arrived to prevent anyone from leaving.

I got there and found my son crying hysterically, shaking, and hyperventilating. He had just told the police about his dad and that his dad was wrong.

The cop responded, "Two wrongs don't make a right."

It got progressively worse. I explained my position, what I do as an advocate. Our therapy dog, a pug named Lily, was going crazy. I showed them the documents that proved I have a protected address. I was calm. The police remained polite until the female sergeant arrived.

At first, I was relieved that a woman had arrived. I thought maybe she would understand. I was wrong. She was not polite at all. She treated me like a hardened criminal.

My child was clinging to me with all his strength.

"Your child is going," she said.

I tried to explain our situation again. I showed her our confidential address and about eight orders of protection that had been issued year after year. She didn't care.

"Ma'am, I'm going to cuff you and arrest you if you don't give me the child."

She was cold and demeaning. *Nasty.*

"Can't you see the condition your child is in?" She shoved paperwork at me.

The Parkersburg West Virginia police were there. CPS was there. Sgt. Nasty was there.

These people were human beings, I knew that. But at that moment, I looked around and saw a group of Stepford wives—robots doing their job without empathy, without compassion. The sounds of my child begging for my protection echoed in my ears and branded my heart.

She had one of her officers put me in handcuffs. Yes, she cuffed me in front of my crying, devastated child. The CPS worker put him in the backseat of a police car. I watched as he pressed his hands against the window, crying for me as the car drove away.

It was the absolute worst moment of my life.

The Next Days

I stayed up and prayed for my son all night long. I later learned that he was taken to a CPS safe house. Rick illegally crossed state lines to pick him up. His girlfriend, with two DWIs herself, drove them back to New York.

I discovered that Sgt. Nasty had been suspended in 2015 for going off on a fourteen-year-old who had recorded her saying every word you can imagine. The sergeant reported that I had coached Christian to cry crocodile tears. That wasn't even possible because I wasn't there. A friend had recorded a video of the incident that added evidence that she was lying.

The Parkersville Police Department made a public apology for her behavior in the 2015 incident and claimed they would learn from the incident. Clearly, they did not. It is amazing the fights we parents must go through. She also said that I was crying hysterically. That is also proven false by the video. My own attorney was blown away at how I acted. He gave me props and told me he respected me. That's the way I was during the entire incident.

Now, I am a patriot and I love the police. However, the police need to learn how to de-escalate a situation because people, especially children, react in dramatic ways when they feel trauma or threatened. That doesn't mean that they are resisting arrest necessarily, if that makes sense.

Police officers need to know how to enter intense situations and hear people out like human beings instead of becoming reactionary themselves. I have watched a police officer transform from a human being into a robot in a split second. I believe they are so brainwashed, so controlled by their jobs, that they lose sight of who they are. They get their paychecks and go home. They really are like puppets. It's quite sad because they often have the power to do something to help.

And I see CPS making the same mistakes because they are not taking the time to make sure their information is accurate and proper. Like the police, they forget to be human when dealing with people who feel threatened.

My Day in Court

After years of going to court to protect my child, I found myself facing charges for the first time. I was charged with contempt of court for failing to make an appearance in court and not obeying the court's decision to give my son to Rick. Of course, since I wasn't served in these matters, I couldn't possibly have responded.

The process server testified that he had left papers taped to my mother's door because she was my designated agent. He kept referring to his notes to get his *facts* right. Then, my mother was called to testify.

Her testimony, excerpted from court records:[7]*

> *I woke up, got out of bed, I opened my window, and this gentleman was outside, and he asked if I was (name omitted) and I said, "Yes."*
>
> *And he says, "I have something for you."*
>
> *And I say, "Well, who are you?" He gave me no information.*

She then stated that she had put on her bathrobe and slippers and gone downstairs to open the door. He, the process server, was standing there.

> *He was standing there, and he handed me papers. He had several papers in his hands. I asked him who he was. I asked him what all this was about and he says, "I'm just here to give you this." I am standing there with the screen door opened and the inside door, and I was inside and he was outside. I asked him who he was. He gave me no information. I had no idea. He didn't say, "I'm a process server."*
>
> *I looked at the top of the paper and it had Rick's name, and on the bottom, it said Frances Amato, so I said, "We'll, I'm neither of these people. This is my home. Frances Amato is my daughter, but why are you giving this to me?"*
>
> *And he said, "Well, they're . . . I was told to give them to you."*

---

7   *Testimony and questions in this section based on Ulster County, New York, court records V-2538-08/17CG

And I said, "Well, I don't know why, and I don't know where my daughter is, and you woke me up at 6:30 in the morning. Please leave." I gave him the papers back, and I was about to close the door, and he threw them in the street. Then, he got in his car and left.

Then, it was my turn to testify. No matter how my attorney tried to ask questions about the choices I had made in the past weeks, the objections to the questions were always sustained. He was not allowed to ask me about orders of protection or about my son begging me not to send him back.

Mr. Gilday, Rick's public defender, kept asking me questions about my job and location, asking me to violate the terms of my confidential address. When I told the court my reason for not divulging the specifics of my work and its locations, Gilday asked for a negative inference by the judge. He wanted the court to believe I was hiding incriminating details, instead of protecting my well-being and my family.

"When you found out there had been a change in custody, did you take steps to return your son to his father?" he asked me.

"I took legal steps to do the right thing to protect my son," I replied.

"Did you take the child and bring him to his father?"

I answered, "I fear for my child in his father's care."

"You didn't want to give your child back to his father, did you?"

"It was never back," I answered. "It was never back. He's never had him."

"You didn't want to give the child to his father." This time it was not a question.

"No." I said, "My child is endangered every time he's there, so no."

"The answer is no. And there was no way you were going to give your child back to his father, was there?"

"I was trying to go through court to get this settled properly, so he would be safe."

That was the truth, the whole truth, so help me God. I had a new attorney who was working quickly to set things right.

Then, he asked me about the day they came and took my son. "You didn't want Christian to go, did you?"

I countered with my own question, "Do you know any normal mother that would want her child to go into abuse?"

Then he brought up that I was placed in handcuffs during the horrible day. "Isn't it true that the Parkersburg police had to place you in handcuffs?"

"Yes," I replied, "in front of my child, they put me in handcuffs."

"And you were complaining to the police that you didn't want Christian to leave?"

"Well, while the child was clinging to me, screaming, hyperventilating, and shaking and not wanting to go, his mother, who loves him very much and takes impeccable care of him . . ."

"And you didn't want him to go."

". . .also, didn't want him to go."

"So, they had to place you in handcuffs."

"That was much later on. I wasn't kicking and screaming and foaming from the mouth. I remained calm through the whole thing. And I was only in handcuffs for about two minutes. They put them on and then took them right off."

He changed the line of questioning and tried to prove that I *moved* out of state because I travel to different locations for my advocacy work. I left the state for work and vacation time, but I lived, and still live, in Ulster County.

Finally, we got to the heart of the matter. After I stated that Christian and I were both victims of domestic violence, he asked, "And all of that gives you the right to supersede court orders?"

"I'm not superseding any court orders."

"What are you doing?"

"I'm not superseding—this—the court order is actually endangering the welfare of my child and myself."

"Ergo, you don't follow it, right?"

"No," I argued, "that's not true, because I've been trying to follow it for nine years, but every time my child comes back—and I can start telling you some stories about the damages that it's caused my child for nine years . . ."

"And *you* know better . . ." he said.

"And the court has completely ignored the evidence that has been presented into this court repeatedly about the damages that have occurred to my child and to myself for nine years. It gets to you after a while."

"And so, after a while, would it be fair to say that you do what you want to do?"

"I've *never* been able to do what I want to do. Our lives have been in shambles, thanks to what has happened in this court for almost a decade."

"So, the orders of the court are irrelevant to you? Which is more important? A court order or protecting your child?" he asked.

"Is a court order more important than the protection of my child? That question puts me in a very difficult place as a mother, a law-abiding mother."

"If you're law-abiding, why don't you follow the law?"

I drew in my breath and spoke the truth. "Because the protection of my child comes before anything. If a truck were coming at my child, I would move him out of the way. But if the judge says to me that I've got to stand there and keep him in front of that truck as it aims for him, what would I do? I'm going to move my child out of the way. And I moved my child out of the way."

The Sentence

The judge ruled that my mother, as my agent, had been properly served. He said that he resolved all discrepancies in testimony in favor of Mr. M (process server). Just like that, he called my seventy-three-year-old mother a liar.

He ruled that there was a lawful order of court that I was to surrender Christian to Rick, and that I disobeyed that order and had established all the elements of civil contempt.

And then he rendered his verdict:

> *The Court's orders must be vindicated. No one, no parent, however concerned they are about the safety of their child, has any right to disobey a clear and unequivocal court order. No one has that right. And her violation of court orders has been flagrant, have been repeated, have been intentional*
> (Ulster county court record, V-2538-08/17CG).

He sentenced me to a full sentence of sixty days in jail for contempt of court. I was taken into custody.

Jail

I went out to the corrections van in my *court* clothes, a Calvin Klein suit and heels.

The officer took one look at me and said, "I'm not cuffing your ankles, but I have to cuff your arms."

He cuffed them in front even though he was supposed to cuff them behind me.

As we rode to lockup, I could hear them asking each other, "What the fuck is this shit? Why is she here?"

I was processed at the jail. Honestly, it was disgusting. I had always obeyed the laws of God and my country, but here I was. I was placed in a holding cell alone, away from the general prison population. In holding, I met a nineteen-year-old-woman, and we talked a lot. My story spread throughout the facility, the story of a mother in jail for protecting her child.

I slept quite a bit, off and on. I was exhausted, my battle lost for the day.

I was taken into custody on January 31, the day after my birthday.

My attorney filed for my sentence to be stayed or vacated with the New York Supreme Court. He argued that the reason people go to jail for contempt is to make them obey the court. My son was with his father already. There was nothing I could do. That made my sentence *punishment*, which is not what contempt sentences are designed to do.

He argued that the judge sentenced me just to punish me and that was an abuse of discretion. The Supreme Court agreed with my lawyer. On February 2, I was released and walked out of jail less than two days after I arrived.

As I was leaving, the other inmates stood and clapped for me. Like I said, my story had been going around the jail.

"Never come back," they shouted, joking with me.

Then they told me to go get my child. "Bless you, Mama," they said as I walked out.

Supervised Visits

I was out of jail, but still imprisoned by the injustice system that had stolen my son. I was granted two hours of supervised visits with my son each week. Supervised visits, like Rick was granted the first time we went to court.

I went. Of course, I went. During these visits, our supervisor noted that our visits went well, and that Christian was happy with me there. Then, he began to share stories of what was happening to him at his father's place. He cried during these visits and begged to come *home*. The supervisor heard these things, but refused to report them.

I pressed her to report to CPS what my child was sharing. In response, she refused to supervise our visits any further. I had no further contact with my son at all. It was hell. I couldn't imagine what it was like for my son.

Part VI

HOPE

In My Corner

Peace from God

And the peace of God,
which transcends all understanding,
will guide your heart and mind in Christ Jesus.
—Philippians 4:7, NIV

There is a natural side and a spiritual side in each of us, right?

I have been through stuff less difficult than this. I have been shaken all over. My natural side has felt anxiety and fear. But, I have been a Christian all these years, and I am more seasoned now. My spiritual side knows this peace of Christ, and this place of peace is greater than my natural side.

Every once in a while, I will burst out in anger, but I still have that place of peace in my heart. We all relate to others through our own relationship to the Lord our God. No matter how they act or react, we can respond from a place of peace.

I think of Jesus when he was annoyed and took out the whip against the money changers and the gamblers in the temple in Jerusalem. I am sure he remained in perfect peace when he did that.

When you are angry, you know if that anger is really a wicked or unrighteous anger. You know if that anger is righteous. And righteous anger comes with a lot of authority.

Does that make sense to you?

During this time without my son, I experienced tremendous pain and anger, but the intense peace in my heart stayed with me. I couldn't explain it if I tried. It was amazing. I was at peace while feeling the natural pain of it all.

Declare the Word

If you are in a place of righteous anger, go through the Bible and collect all the scriptures you can find. Search for scriptures about the promises of God. In your horrible storm, look for scriptures that lead you to say *yes* and *amen*. In God, *no* and *maybe* don't exist. Even if you are seeing no way out and don't know how your life can be right again, go find a promise of God.

God wants us to live a healthy, happy, safe life. He wants us to sleep the sweet sleep of happiness. He does not want us to be tossed about. He does not want children to be abused.

Look until you find a promise. Find your *yes* and *amen*. You must name them.

When the Marlboro police came after me to take me to court, they were amazed at how I handled it. My first reaction was fear and then I told myself *no*. Instead I said, "Greater is He that is in me, than he that is in the world (I John 4:4, KJV)." I just kept saying it. I only had to say it three times before the peace crept up inside me.

Years ago, I would have had to say it at least fifty times. Now, I believe those words immediately, and God takes over my body so that I can feel His peace. You can feel His peace, too, and know that He is with you. Nobody—no court, no judge—can take that away from you.

We began a twenty-four-hour prayer vigil for Christian after he was taken from me, consciously speaking the Word over him every day.

Love and Support

When Rick posted that Christian and I were missing, the support began to pour in. People were ripping down the posters, and I even received messages from some of Rick's friends who apologized for helping him.

When people saw my Facebook video of my son crying not to be taken away from me, they reached out to me in many ways: emails, calls, and Facebook messages. They all told me they were sorry. They realized that just like the evening news, what is reported is not always correct.

They took the time to find out what was really going on. It was like somebody kidnapped a child. Our story was absurd, over the top. When they learned the truth, they would say, "Oh my gosh, we didn't know." Craziness!

These were not strangers coming out of the woodwork. The people from Kingston who were actually part of Rick's circle began to apologize to me. *What can we do? We are praying for you.* They would tell me their horror stories about Ulster County family court. They began to tell me that they would not tolerate this. This is the community, the town, I was pretty much raised in. It raised my spirit to see their support.

Then, it was like a million people from everywhere started praying around the clock. I started receiving messages morning, noon, and night. My inbox on Facebook was constantly dinging, as were my email and phone. People informing me that they would be praying at twelve o'clock, at 2:00 a.m., in the middle of the day, praying for Christian and they spoke the Word.

I saw how people really are—wonderful and loving and caring. It helped me get through.

My family is amazing. My sister, Toni, and my mother did everything they possibly could. My aunts and uncles, the friends I grew up with, Kathy and Christine—all of them couldn't do enough for me. It helped me get through.

Additionally, there were people that I didn't even know liked me. Suddenly they were hugging me and telling me how sorry they were with tears in their eyes.

You are the last person who deserves this, they whispered.

Some broken relationships healed as people came forward to support me, and friendships were mended.

Because these people came together, I felt loved and supported.

Even in my struggle, I thought: *Wow! This is pretty cool.*

A Small Miracle

I honestly did not have money for a lawyer. A lot of people are completely bankrupted by the abuse from family court. I know tons of people like that. I wasn't bankrupt, but I didn't have the money it was going to cost to fight for my son. So, I did a GoFundMe campaign.

The GoFundMe campaign had raised some money, mainly from our close family and friends who had made individual contributions. Then, Rick and his paramour, who is another loaded gun, had it taken down after just a couple of days. They reported that there was a warrant out for my arrest.

I needed a lawyer to fix the mess I was in and to keep a strong watch on the wickedness of this particular family court. I was faced with a court that types their own version of transcripts, falsifies records, doesn't bring in evidence or ask the right questions. I needed somebody to fight for me.

I still needed a significant sum of money. Overnight, it was paid by someone willing to support my fight. It is amazing that God just turned the situation right around. He is the one source you can trust to give you more than you need. So, whatever is being used for evil, God will turn around for His good and His glory.

He did. He just did it. I was encouraged. I was not encouraged by the fact my son was still in danger. I still asked God why He was allowing my child to be in that place. But, I had witnessed a miracle, so I prayed for another miracle to happen for my son. I prayed for all the parents whose children were in danger. Prayer is the way to get things done. Prayer combats the evil attacking these kids, all these kids. It just breaks my heart.

The Prayer Warriors

People were praying for me around the clock—in the middle of the night, taking different shifts. They were praying for Christian's safety. They were praying for this judge to be removed or arrested. I knew something would happen. In the moments when I was down, not feeling hopeful, I could feel their prayers.

One prayer warrior, my good friend Dawn Ranco, sent me this Word:

The giant will come down! Stand tall, Sister.

There's much to be said, and you will say it. You will speak under the authority of the Almighty!

You will stand in the face of the giant and will have an anointed word upon your lips.

You will speak not with the lips of Fran, but with the lips of God of All Authority, speaking righteousness!

There are many that have been broken under the feet of the unrighteous. But now, eyes are upon you, and they will see and know that there is an authority of all. Not man-made, with hands of flesh. But, with the fire of hot coals off the altar.

Anointed by the Holy Ghost—a mere woman, they say, what will and can she do? They will see and know something was profoundly done.

You are a vessel unto honor, and I have sheltered you and my son under the shadow of my wings.

I am God, always will be God!

And, no weapon formed against you shall prosper. Stand tall in your anointing. I have told you many times I AM YOUR FATHER!

I will never leave you or forsake you.

I will uphold you.

I will send you comforters of the Holy Spirit.

I know your flesh wants to rear up and take matters into your own hands, because of your and your family's hurts.

I know your brokenness when you're alone and missing your baby. I am with you. You're not alone.

I have told you, child, that I am working even when you think I'm not.

You have favor, whereby other people work tirelessly on your behalf. They even question themselves, as to why they are doing so much for you. It is because of me, your Heavenly Father!

Your son, being a child, and acting as a child, is very wise in his young years. He sees the truth, knows the truth, speaks the truth. And it is because of your faithfulness, you not wavering from the truth, that much was done and instilled in him—my characteristic of righteousness. He will say and do more than you realize.

A young Daniel in a lion's den. He is watched over by the Lion of Judah!

Rest in me, dear daughter. People are watching your action from afar. Run to the cross and to your inner circle to allow your flesh to vent.

Pray with the fire of the Holy Ghost for the flesh to be burnt up. And then, be restored with the strength of God and the anointing of your Holy God.

Much is said in your quietness before me. Whereby, I speak in silent action for others to behold God's Glory!

Be still in flesh, knowing your God lives.

See through your eyes of faith.

Trust in the God you serve.

The very ones who separated from you and were led by your acts of flesh will see: I leave the ninety-nine for the one, when their trust is in me.

Be continually armed with the armor of God and in the actions of the Holy Spirit.

Let it be less of you! More of me! Key people will see more of me if their total trust is in me, Almighty God.

Be wise as a serpent, and gentle as a dove.

Your fight does not come from being Italian, but by being a flesh-brought child of God.

Sit in awe and be amazed of how much is done under and through the Holy Ghost.

Rest in me, being on guard through prayer and supplication.

Keep a watchman over your mouth until you are led to speak.

Be still and know me, my child.

Amen. I am your God.

Walk Right Through Hell
Yea, though I walk through the valley of the shadow of death,
I will fear no evil, for thou art with me.

—Psalm 23: 4, KJB

I was walking through hell and perhaps you are, too. If you are a mother or father who has lost her child, you fear nothing. Your worst fear has come to pass. You simply move through your day.

I was feeling as if my house was on fire, but I couldn't rescue my child from the flames. I kept my eyes on the Lord and on my child, believing I would come out on the other side.

You will come out on the other side. You will be rescued. And that is what I see.

Glimmers of Hope

Think of Martin Luther King Jr. Think of Sojourner Truth. Think of those people who impacted our world today even with the odds stacked against them. Looking at them should give you a glimmer of hope. They certainly brought hope to me.

I worked with my Assemblyman Frank Skartados and his chief of staff, Steve Gold. Our work was a glimmer of hope.

I helped legislators write *Mason's Law*, outlining mandated reporting for symptoms and reports of abuse. I started my coalition in New York and expanded. Our state was a glimmer of hope.

When we act against the wrongs we see, we are a glimmer of hope. This book is a glimmer of hope as it will provide exposure not just for me, but for thousands of people here in our own country.

There are children in this country who have been failed by this system who need that hope. There are parents who haven't told their stories who need that hope. Maybe you need that hope.

We want things to be made right again. We want to strengthen our resolve. We want to see justice served. Together, we are all a glimmer of hope.

Don't Back Down

Life in the Void

For months, I did not see my son. I did not stop working.

The coalition work continued, getting stronger each day. We formed the National Coalition for Family Court and CPS Reform. We started a website, punished4beingaparent. com. From that website came our new talk show, "Punished 4 Protecting," that broadcasts over the web. Our base of support grew as did our influence.

We kept sending advocates to court-watch, to take notes and be a support system to good parents who were struggling.

I kept going to court, trying to get my son back. I tried to break the legal hold on our lives.

Rick wound up in jail for a short time in June 2017 and contacted an advocate who filed a sworn affidavit trying to protect my son and me:

Rick . . . admitted to me that he knows he has a drug and alcohol problem and that he has no home for him or the child. As an advocate and as an ethical person, it concerned me that Rick said the child attorney (Amy Ingram) told him she will work to get custody to his mother and sister . . . He also admitted that the child has been crying for his mother and his home . . .[8*]

Of course, the judge ignored this statement. Everything continued down the same path: I would produce evidence, and the judge would ignore it. Until . . .

The Best Day

Rick broke his probation and wound up in jail again. We had an upcoming court date and found out that Rick's sister had also filed for sole custody of Christian as Rick would be in jail for a year.

When we arrived at the court building on Tuesday morning, September 12, 2017, we first went into a conference room to pray. My new attorney, Steven Klein, prayed with me and my family. We braced for the worst.

In the hearing room, we introduced ourselves. Rick was on the phone from jail. He explained to the judge how the things he did weren't really wrong. Some things never change, I guess. Ms. Ingram informed the court that Christian would

---

8   * Name withheld by request

like to stay with his aunt for the year it would take for Rick to be released from jail.

We made our case, the same case we had made for all these years. I had always been Christian's primary caregiver, and as his mother, I simply wanted to continue to do what I had always done. My attorney read my statement to the judge.

We were all dismissed to the lobby while the judge deliberated. In the lobby, my attorney handed Amy Ingram a letter from the New York State Supreme Court, informing her that she was being relieved of her duties as Christian's attorney for the child. Her pattern of lying about what children say and what they want had cost us so much.

My sister and I, tired of being polite in the face of abuse, spoke loudly enough for everyone to hear.

"She's such a liar, that woman," I said. "I'm so sick of that woman," I spoke to the room.

Mr. Gilday returned the favor. "That whole family is the same. They are all like HER."

I was happy to respond, "Yes, I'm just like my sister, Toni. She's a best-selling author and nutritionist who helps people get well from cancer." It was Toni's birthday that day, and I was proud to be compared to her.

We were called back into court.

In a simple statement, Judge McGinty gave me sole custody of my son.

I was overwhelmed, bursting into tears. I sobbed with the sweetest relief that my boy was coming home to me, to my protection, to my life.

My family exploded in gratitude to the very judge who had wreaked such pain in our lives.

"Thank you," they kept repeating, until he made them stop.

We left the courthouse with light feet and waited until our attorney brought us the paper that would allow me to pick Christian up from school. The paper that was my release from this unjust prison.

Reunion

We all went to Christian's school with balloons and happy hearts. The principal, however, was not pleased to see us. She called us immature and informed us that our *family reunion* was not appropriate. We caught her on our live Facebook feed. Two thousand irate people have contacted the school to complain about her behavior. To me, it didn't matter what she said because inside I was jumping for joy!

We discovered later that she allowed Rick's sister to pull my son out of class, illegally, to say goodbye. Perhaps this part of the story isn't quite over.

It was my sister's birthday, so my family celebrated together all day. I received an email from my book editor saying that she was with my publishers and they were all doing a happy dance, celebrating a happy ending to my book and our work together. It was perfect.

However, the toll of this journey on my son and my family is huge. He has done nothing but talk about how terrible his life was with his father. He reports one crazy thing after another. He tells me how the noise kept him up all hours of the night until he was exhausted at school.

He told me that his uncle, the drug dealer, had come home to his grandfather's house while Christian was visiting. The uncle had started beating the grandfather. Christian and his cousin ran to a neighbor's house for help, but no one made a call. No one helped these two boys. My son was never supposed to be at this residence in the first place because the uncle lived there.

I know he will tell me more horror stories.

I know more parents will share their pain, their horror stories, too. My book has a happy ending, but my work continues.

Forward!

Action Steps

Have you heard the saying: *You may have lost the battle, but that doesn't mean you have lost the war?*

If you are fighting for your children, I want you to stay in the fight. Don't lose hope. The war isn't over.

The victory can be yours. There really isn't another option when your child is involved, is there? Keep your focus and stay in the fight to win the safety and protection of your family, your children. If you quit, it will turn people off who might help you. Period. It is your God-given right to protect and parent your children. Don't forget that.

I hope that my story encourages you to act and to act now. Get out your pen and paper and make notes. There are many things you can do.

Contact us at the National Coalition for Family Court and CPS Reform. Contact the U.S. Department of Justice.

Contact the FBI. Tell your story in every place you can, and don't do it alone.

Strategize for maximum impact. Set up strategic meetings with other people who are going through the same situation. Write letters and make calls together. Pool your information and combine it to send to the DOJ, FBI, local senators, your governor, assemblymen, and other legislators so that a complete change can be made and this injustice is completely turned around. Find advocacy groups for domestic violence or for whatever issue you are facing. Get the troops together.

Once again, if you are working with a group, you can create a powerful voice when you act together. Develop a strategy. For example, decide that everyone in the group is going to call the Department of Justice on Monday and the FBI on Tuesday. If need be, rent a van or a bus and travel to the offices of these organizations or politicians. File your complaints in larger numbers to attract the attention of the people you need to help you.

Organize a peaceful demonstration and exercise your first-amendment right to freedom of speech. Assemble in front of the office of Child Protective Services, or whatever the organization is called in your state. Gather in an organized, peaceful fashion. That way, when the news crews show up, you are articulating the crimes being committed, the civil liberties being violated, and the Americans with Disabilities

Act (ADA) rights that are being violated. This exposure will spread your concerns to the public eye as much as possible.

The way you handle yourself is very important. Let the cameras and the public see who they are dealing with—decent, hardworking human beings who are suffering. Help them see that the stigma of people losing their children needs to be changed—that you are not talking about parents who are shooting heroin in the corner of a park. Remember, you are exposing the truth to change an entire system of injustice.

Support yourself and others. Find trusting friends and fellowships. This can include counseling groups where you sit with one another to build and hold each other up. That support system is important because it will keep you from losing who you are, so that you don't believe the lies you are being fed. In these groups, you receive help to hold true to who you are as a human being, and you will help others do that as well.

Hire an attorney if you can, and make sure you do your homework. Your attorney must understand domestic violence and child abuse. They need to be privy to laws in these areas as well.

You may think: *Does she need to say that?*

Yes, I do. A lot of attorneys are not up to speed in these areas.

Put your nose in books. Learn about the role of a child attorney in your state and the training required. Read and take notes while you read about the ethical expectations of lawyers who represent children in the system. Share your notes with your attorney. Don't assume that your lawyer knows everything you find.

Use caution if you are assigned an attorney connected to the court. They do not always act with integrity or fight for you in the right way. You want the right one.

Learn about federal laws. Make sure you know the family court laws in your state. You may find that these laws represent your own moral compass. You will be encouraged when you realize that the laws actually confirm that you are right 99.9 percent of the time. Don't let a corrupt system tell you that you are wrong when the law backs you up.

Research the work done by experts in the field that will back you up while helping you learn how to care for your child.

Resources:

- The Saunders Study can be found at ncjrs.gov/pdffiles1/nij/grants/238891.pdf.

- ACEs (Adverse Childhood Experiences) report findings at cdc.gov/violenceprevention/acestudy/index.html.

- ADA (Americans with Disabilities Act) at ada.gov.

Create a paper trail. When you go to court, take notes. Read the transcripts and note page numbers of anything stated incorrectly. Transcripts are sometimes fudged or transcribed incorrectly. Records are falsified. Have an advocate go to court with you to also take notes. They won't be required to pay attention to anything except the details of what is happening.

Know your rights. CPS is not allowed in your home without a warrant. You don't have to let them in. Take back what belongs to you. Be forthright and state when your rights are being violated.

Live Right and do no wrong. If you are using drugs, drinking alcohol, and abusing others, you will not find an advocacy center that will support you unless you get help. If you have issues, you need to admit them.

If you are a person who doesn't do these things and your rights are being violated, then you need to be in the company of like-minded parents. If your children are being endangered, make sure your background stays clean and that you associate with others who are protective parents, living a law-abiding life.

Care for yourself. Eat good meals and get enough sleep. Strengthen your body for the fight because you know you are fighting to win. Work on being healthy.

If you have an addiction problem, seek the help you need and allow your children time to experience you as a healthy, caring person. Be fair to them as you are fair to yourself. Unless you fight first for them by improving your own health, an advocate won't fight for you.

My Promise

I am a mother in the true sense of the word, and I don't know any other true mothers who would ever back down from protecting their children. Recently, I attended an event for *One Billion Rising,* a day of global action and dancing to protest violence against women. I watched their video and saw mothers whose children were taken for no reason.

In the video, the women say, "We are here one billion strong, protecting our children can never be wrong."

It is crazy that we need to say those words out loud, isn't it?

How can I back down from that?

These courts need to be not only exposed, but admonished and punished for the crimes they are committing.

I promise that as long as a child needs to be protected from a dangerous place, I will never back down.

I promise that as long as there is another opportunity to do something else on the side of what is right, I will never back down.

I promise to work to build a support system that spreads into every county in this country so that no good parent is alone in the fight.

Those are my promises, but remember that this fight also falls on you.

So, you can never back down either. You cannot ever back down.

APPENDIX

A parent's right to the preservation of his relationship with his child derives from the fact that the parent's achievement of a rich and rewarding life is likely to depend significantly on his ability to participate in the rearing of his offspring. A child's corresponding right to protection from interference in the relationship derives from the psychic importance to him of being raised by a loving, responsible, reliable adult.

> *Franz v. United States*, 707 F. 2d 582, 599
> (D.C. Cir. 1983)

Since custody and visitation encompass practically all of what we call "parental rights," a total denial of both would be the equivalent of termination of parental rights.

> *Franz v. United States*, 707 F. 2d 582, 602
> (D.C. Cir.1983)

The rights of parents to the care, custody, and nurture of their children is of such character that it cannot be denied without violating those fundamental principles of liberty and justice which lie at the base of all our civil and political institutions, and such right is a fundamental right protected by this amendment (First) and Amendments 5, 9, and 14.

> *Doe v. Irwin*, 441 F Supp 1247 (D. Mich.1985)

The several states have no greater power to restrain individual freedoms protected by the First Amendment than does the Congress of the United States.

Wallace v. Jaffree, 105 S Ct 2479; 472 U.S. 38 (1985)

Loss of First Amendment Freedoms, for even minimal periods of time, unquestionably constitutes irreparable injury. Though First Amendment rights are not absolute, they may be curtailed only by interests of vital importance, the burden of proving which rests on their government.

Elrod v. Burns, 96 S Ct 2673; 427 U.S. 347 (1976)

Law and court procedures that are "fair on their faces" but administered "with an evil eye or a heavy hand" are discriminatory and violate the equal protection clause of the Fourteenth Amendment.

Yick Wo v. Hopkins, 118 U.S. 356 (1886)

Even when blood relationships are strained, parents retain vital interest in preventing irretrievable destruction of their family life; if anything, persons faced with forced dissolution of their parental rights have more critical need for procedural protections than do those resisting state intervention into ongoing family affairs.

Santosky v. Kramer, 102 S Ct 1388; 455 U.S. 745 (1982)

The liberty interest of the family encompasses an interest in retaining custody of one's children and, thus, a state may not interfere with a parent's custodial rights absent due process protections.

Langton v. Maloney, 527 F Supp 538, D.C. Conn. (1981)

Parent's right to custody of child is a right encompassed within protection of this amendment which may not be interfered with under guise of protecting public interest by legislative action which is arbitrary or without reasonable relation to some purpose within competency of state to effect.

Reynold v. Baby Fold, Inc., 369 NE 2d 858; 68 Ill 2d 419, appeal dismissed 98 S Ct 1598, 435 U.S. 963, IL (1977)

Parent's interest in custody of her children is a liberty interest which has received considerable constitutional protection; a parent who is deprived of custody of his or her child, even though temporarily, suffers thereby grievous loss and such loss deserves extensive due process protection.

In the Interest of Cooper, 621 P 2d 437; 5 Kansas App Div 2d 584 (1980)

The Due Process Clause of the Fourteenth Amendment requires that severance in the parent-child relationship caused by the state occur only with rigorous protections for individual liberty interests at stake.

Bell v. City of Milwaukee, 746 F. 2d 1205
(7th Cir. Wisc. 1984)

Father enjoys the right to associate with his children which is guaranteed by this amendment (First) as incorporated in Amendment 14, or which is embodied in the concept of "liberty" as that word is used in the Due Process Clause of the 14th Amendment and Equal Protection Clause of the 14th Amendment.

Mabra v. Schmidt, 356 F Supp 620 (D. Wisc. 1973)

The United States Supreme Court noted that a parent's right to "the companionship, care, custody and management of his or her children" is an interest "far more precious" than any property right.

May v. Anderson, 345 U.S. 528, 533; 73 S Ct 840, 843
(1952)

A parent's right to care and companionship of his or her children are so fundamental, as to be guaranteed protection under the First, Ninth, and Fourteenth Amendments of the United States Constitution.

In re J.S. and C., 324 A. 2d 90; 129 N.J.
Super. 486, 489–492 (1974)

The Court stressed, "the parent-child relationship is an important interest that undeniably warrants deference and, absent a powerful countervailing interest, protection." A parent's interest in the companionship, care, custody and management of his or her children rises to a constitutionally secured right, given the centrality of family life as the focus for personal meaning and responsibility.

Stanley v. Illinois, 405 U.S. 645, 651; 92 S Ct 1208 (1972)

The U.S. Supreme Court implied that "a (once) married father who is separated or divorced from a mother and is no longer living with his child" could not constitutionally be treated differently from a currently married father living with his child.

Quilloin v. Walcott, 98 S Ct 549;
434 U.S. 246, 255–56 (1978)

The U.S. Court of Appeals for the 9th Circuit (California) held that the parent-child relationship is a constitutionally protected liberty interest. (See; *Declaration of Independence* — life, liberty and the pursuit of happiness and the 14th Amendment of the United States Constitution — No state can deprive any person of life, liberty or property without due process of law nor deny any person the equal protection of the laws.)

Kelson v. Springfield, 767 F. 2d 651 (9th Cir. 1985)

The parent-child relationship is a liberty interest protected by the Due Process Clause of the 14th Amendment.

Bell v. City of Milwaukee, 746 F. 2d 1205, 1242–45 (7th Cir. Wisc. 1985)

"No bond is more precious and none should be more zealously protected by the law as the bond between parent and child."

Carson v. Elrod, 411 F. Supp. 645, 649 (E.D. Va. 1976)

A parent's right to the preservation of his relationship with his child derives from the fact that the parent's achievement of a rich and rewarding life is likely to depend significantly on his ability to participate in the rearing of his children. A child's corresponding right to protection from interference in the relationship derives from the psychic importance to him of being raised by a loving, responsible, reliable adult.

Franz v. U.S., 707 F. 2d 582, 595–599 (D.C. Cir. 1983)

A parent's right to the custody of his or her children is an element of "liberty" guaranteed by the 5th Amendment and the 14th Amendment of the United States Constitution.

Matter of Gentry, 369 NW 2d 889, Mich. App. Div. (1983)

Reality of private biases and possible injury they might inflict were impermissible considerations under the Equal Protection Clause of the 14th Amendment.

Palmore v. Sidoti, 104 S Ct 1879, 466 U.S. 429 (1984)

Legislative classifications which distribute benefits and burdens on the basis of gender carry the inherent risk of reinforcing stereotypes about the proper place of women and their need for special protection; thus, even statutes purportedly designed to compensate for and ameliorate the effects of past discrimination against women must be carefully tailored. The state cannot be permitted to classify on the basis of sex.

Orr v. Orr, 99 S. Ct. 1102 (1979)

The United States Supreme Court held that the "old notion" that "generally it is the man's primary responsibility to provide a home and its essentials" can no longer justify a statute that discriminates on the basis of gender. No longer is the female destined solely for the home and the rearing of the family, and only the male for the marketplace and the world of ideas.

Stanton v. Stanton, 421 U.S. 7, 10;
95 S Ct 1373, 1376 (1975)

Judges must maintain a high standard of judicial performance with particular emphasis upon conducting litigation with scrupulous fairness and impartiality.

> 28 USCA § 455. *Pfizer v. Lord*, 456 F. 2d 532; certiorari denied 92 S. Ct. 2411; U.S. Ct App MN (1972)

State Judges, as well as federal, have the responsibility to respect and protect persons from violations of federal constitutional rights.

> *Goss v. State of Illinois*, 312 F. 2d 257 (7th Cir. 1963)

The Constitution also protects "the individual interest in avoiding disclosure of personal matters." Federal Courts (and State Courts), under Griswold can protect, under the "life, liberty and pursuit of Happiness" phrase of the Declaration of Independence, the right of a man to enjoy the mutual care, company, love, and affection of his children, and this cannot be taken away from him without due process of law. There is a family right to privacy which the state cannot invade or it becomes actionable for civil rights damages.

> *Griswold v. Connecticut*, 381 U.S. 479 (1965)

The right of a parent not to be deprived of parental rights without a showing of fitness, abandonment or substantial neglect is so fundamental and basic as to rank among the rights contained in this Amendment (Ninth) and Utah's Constitution, Article 1 § 1.

In re U.P., 648 P.2d 1364 (Utah 1982)

The rights of parents to parent-child relationships are recognized and upheld.

Fantony v. Fantony, 122 A. 2d 593 (N.J. 1956);
Brennan v. Brennan, 454 A. 2d 901 (N.J. 1982)

State's power to legislate, adjudicate and administer all aspects of family law, including determinations of custodial; and visitation rights, is subject to scrutiny by federal judiciary within reach of due process and/ or equal protection clauses of Fourteenth Amendment . . . Fourteenth Amendment applied to states through specific rights contained in the first eight amendments of the Constitution which declares fundamental personal rights . . . Fourteenth Amendment encompasses and applied to states those preexisting fundamental rights recognized by the Ninth Amendment. The Ninth Amendment acknowledged the prior existence of fundamental rights with it: "The enumeration in the Constitution, of certain rights, shall not be construed to deny or disparage others retained by the people." The United States Supreme Court, in a long line of decisions, has recognized that matters involving marriage, procreation, and the parent-child relationship are among those fundamental "liberty" interests protected by the Constitution. Thus, the decision in *Roe v. Wade*, 410 U.S. 113; 93 S. Ct. 705; 35 L. Ed. 2d 147 (1973), was recently described by the Supreme Court as founded on the "Constitutional underpinning of . . . a recognition that the 'liberty' interests protected by the Due Process Clause of the Fourteenth Amendment includes not only the freedoms explicitly mentioned in the Bill of Rights, but also a freedom of personal choice in certain matters of marriage and family life." The non-custodial divorced parent has no way to implement the constitutionally protected right to maintain a parental relationship with his child except through visitation. To acknowledge the protected status of the relationship as the majority does, and yet deny protection under Title 42 USC § 1983, to visitation, which is the exclusive means of effecting that right, is to negate the right completely.

Wise v. Bravo, 666 F. 2d 1328 (1981)

The United States Supreme Court has held that:

The fundamental theory of liberty upon which all governments in this Union repose excludes any general power of the State to standardize its children by forcing them to accept instruction from public teachers only. The child is not the mere creature of the State; those who nurture him and direct his destiny have the right, coupled with the high duty, to recognize and prepare him for additional obligations.

Pierce v. Society of Sisters, 268 U.S. 510 (1925)

It is cardinal with us that the custody, care and nurture of the child reside first in the parents, whose primary function and freedom include preparation for obligations the state can neither supply nor hinder. . . . It is in recognition of this that these decisions have respected the private realm of family life which the state cannot enter.

Prince v. Commonwealth of Massachusetts,
321 U.S. 158 (1944)

The values of parental direction of the religious upbringing and education of their children in their early and formative years have a high place in our society.

Even more markedly than in Prince, therefore, this case involves the fundamental interest of parents, as contrasted with that of the State, to guide the religious future and education of their children. The history and culture of Western civilization reflect a strong tradition of parental concern for the nurture and upbringing of their children. This primary role of the parents in the upbringing of their children is now established beyond debate as an enduring American tradition.

Wisconsin v. Yoder, 406 U.S. 205 (1972)

This Court has long recognized that freedom of personal choice in matters of marriage and family life is one of the liberties protected by the Due Process Clause of the Fourteenth Amendment.

Cleveland Board of Education v. LaFleur,
414 U.S. 632 (1974)

Our decisions establish that the Constitution protects the sanctity of the family precisely because the institution of the family is deeply rooted in this Nation's history and tradition. It is through the family that we inculcate and pass down many of our most cherished values, moral and cultural.

Moore v. East Cleveland, 431 U.S. 494 (1977)

The liberty interest in family privacy has its source, and its contours are ordinarily to be sought, not in state law, but in intrinsic human rights, as they have been understood in "this Nation's history and tradition."

Smith v. Organization of Foster Families,
431 U.S. 816 (1977)

We have recognized on numerous occasions that the relationship between parent and child is constitutionally protected. We have little doubt that the Due Process Clause would be offended "if a State were to attempt to force the breakup of a natural family, over the objections of the parents and their children, without

some showing of unfitness and for the sole reason
that to do so was thought to be in the children's best
interest."

Quilloin v. Walcott, 434 U.S. 246 (1978)

The law's concept of the family rests on a presumption
that parents possess what a child lacks in maturity,
experience, and capacity for judgment required for
making life's difficult decisions. More important,
historically it has recognized that natural bonds of
affection lead parents to act in the best interests of their
children. The statist notion that governmental power
should supersede parental authority in all cases because
some parents abuse and neglect children is repugnant
to American tradition. Simply because the decision of a
parent is not agreeable to a child or because it involves
risks does not automatically transfer the power to
make that decision from the parents to some agency or
officer of the state.

Parham v. J. R., 442 U.S. 584 (1979)

The fundamental liberty interest of natural parents in the care,
custody, and management of their child does not evaporate
simply because they have not been model parents or have
lost temporary custody of their child to the State. Even when
blood relationships are strained, parents retain a vital interest
in preventing the irretrievable destruction of their family life.

Until the State proves parental unfitness, the child and his parents share a vital interest in preventing erroneous termination of their natural relationship.

Santosky v. Kramer, 455 U.S. 745 (1982)

"The best interests of the child," a venerable phrase familiar from divorce proceedings, is a proper and feasible criterion for making the decision as to which of two parents will be accorded custody. But it is not traditionally the sole criterion-much less the sole constitutional criterion-for other, less narrowly channeled judgments involving children, where their interests conflict in varying degrees with the interests of others.

"The best interests of the child" is not the legal standard that governs parents' or guardians' exercise of their custody: So long as certain minimum requirements of child care are met, the interests of the child may be subordinated to the interests of other children, or indeed even to the interests of the parents or guardians themselves.

Reno v. Flores, 507 U.S. 292 (1993)

In a long line of cases, we have held that, in addition to the specific freedoms protected by the Bill of Rights, the "liberty" specially protected by the Due Process Clause includes the rights . . . to direct the education and upbringing of one's children. The Fourteenth

Amendment "forbids the government to infringe ... 'fundamental' liberty interests of all, no matter what process is provided, unless the infringement is narrowly tailored to serve a compelling state interest."

Washington v. Glucksburg, 521 U.S. 702 (1997)

Next Steps

Visit our website at punished4beingaparent.com where you can watch our TV show, *Punished 4 Protecting*, now broadcasting all over California, Minnesota, and in parts of New York, including Long Island.

You may contact the National Coalition for Family Court and CPS Reform directly at nationalcoalitionfc.cpsreform@yahoo.com.

You may also visit our Facebook page at facebook.com/Punished4Protecting.

We are available to good parents in need of assistance and encourage all good parents to join us in our nationwide efforts to protect our children. We are available for speaking engagements as well.

About the Author

Francesca Amato-Banfield is an advocate, mother, whistleblower, and founder of the National Coalition for Family Court and CPS Reform. She is a noted public speaker who strives to bring attention to the crisis in our family court system here in the United States. As a parental rights and child welfare activist, she has worked closely with legislators to write child protection laws. She has been interviewed by Time Warner Cable, the *Daily Freeman,* and the *Record News.*

She has worked with countless domestic violence and child abuse victims to ensure their safety. She has court-watched the judges in Ulster County and held the first rally for reform in front of Ulster County family court to bring public awareness. For her efforts, she received letters of recognition from her Assemblyman, Frank Skartados.

She began her advocacy work as a chapter leader for the Tri-State Coalition for Court Reform. From there, she expanded her network and reached across the nation. Now, she coordinates advocates across the country. Fran currently hosts and serves as an investigative reporter for her own rapidly expanding television show, *Punished 4 Protecting,* which airs in parts of New York, California, and Minnesota. Since the show's creation in August 2017, she has been a guest on many parental radio shows.

Fran received an associate degree from Mount St. Mary College and has taken adult education in nutrition. She considers herself a true mother—law-abiding and protective—to her children giving them safe stable homes so they can experience the best life offers.

Made in the USA
Coppell, TX
03 May 2020

24116290R00089